KETO

Mediterranean Diet Cookbook 2019

A Ketogenic Solution With 100 Low-carb, High-fat Vibrant

Recipes for Weight Loss, Energy Saving, Busy Schedule,

Delicious Meal and A Mediterranean Lifestyle

Abella Duncan

Legal & Disclaimer

The information and contents herein are not designed to replace or take the place of any form of medical or professional advice and are not meant to replace the need for independent medical, financial, legal or other professional advice or services, as may be required. The content and information in this book have been provided for educational and entertainment purposes only.

The content and information in this book have been compiled from reliable sources and are accurate to the author's best knowledge, information, and belief. The author cannot guarantee this book's accuracy and validity and cannot be held liable for any errors and/or omissions. Further, changes will be periodically made to this book when needed. It is recommended that you consult with a health professional who is familiar with your personal medical history before using any of the suggested remedies, techniques, or information in this book.

Upon using the contents in this book, you agree to hold harmless the author from and against any damages, costs, and expenses, including any legal fees potentially resulting from the application of the information provided You agree to accept all risks associated with using the information presented inside this book.

Content

Chapter 1. The Basics of Mediterranean Diet

What Is the Mediterranean Diet?

Mediterranean diet is a name for food ingredients and recipes involving them used in countries around the Mediterranean sea, such as Croatia and Greece. As different tribes fluctuated into the area, they brought their own recipes and ideas for preparing the food they found: fish, poultry, olives, wheat, fresh fruits, cheese, grapes and yogurt. Local populace voted on the recipes by passing them on, which over centuries resulted in the Mediterranean diet. The diet itself has been protected by UNESCO as cultural heritage. It traditionally uses no eggs, no red meat and just a dash of alcohol, which could explain many health benefits it delivers, such as lowered risk of heart disease.

Benefits of the Mediterranean diet

It appears Mediterranean diet protects against type 2 diabetes, heart disease, weight gain and ballooning waist, most notably due to presence of unsaturated fats from fish and olive oil, lack of processed foods and use of spices instead of salt. Type 2 diabetes is a wicked disease caused by a conglomerate of factors, most of which have to do with diet, almost exclusively affecting Western countries. A type 2 diabetic will generally be overweight with high risk of heart disease, an increased waist circumference and a sedentary lifestyle involving processed sugars, too much salt and saturated fat from red meat. Lifestyle choices and exposure to sun at that latitude add to Mediterranean diet health benefits as well, supplying the person with fresh air, physical activity and vitamin D.

Why is a Mediterranean diet good for you?

A healthy diet is all about making wise choices on a daily basis. Mediterranean diet consists of countless lifetimes of wise choices made by people who wanted to live a long, active and productive life and chose a diet to help them stay fit well into old age. The biggest issues for people in advanced age are chronic weakness, weight gain and lack of mobility, resulting in reliance on their family to remain active. This causes a tremendous amount of stress and anxiety for everyone involved but it doesn't have to be that old people are necessarily quaking and feeble; there's no reason a person can't remain fit and active if fed a proper, nourishing Mediterranean diet.

What makes a Mediterranean diet and lifestyle?

Unsaturated fats from olive oil and omega-3 fatty acids from fish are two key dietary ingredients in the Mediterranean diet; sunshine and vitamin D are two key ingredients for Mediterranean lifestyle. Medicine is still researching why unsaturated fats and omega-3 fatty acids are healthy for the heart but it appears the two lower the amount of bad cholesterol, LDL, and protect arteries from inflammation that leads to atherosclerosis. Heart disease is extremely complex but the root cause seems to be unbalanced diet poor in healthy fats, such as that gotten from vegetables and fish. Sunshine stimulates the circulation and lifts up the mood while vitamin D serves as a protection for the heart and the immune system. These four things – unsaturated fats, omega-3 fatty acids, sunshine and vitamin D – appear to be the healthiest combo for longevity, fitness and good mood.

Keto diet and Mediterranean diet

The definition of the 'ideal' diet keeps changing as more research is carried out. Low-fat diets were formerly trendy until it was discovered that it was not beneficial to health or weight loss. We now know that fat is good.

This article would be comparing the differences and similarities between the ketogenic diet and the Mediterranean diet,

The Ketogenic Diet

Initially created in 1920 as a form of therapy for epileptic children, the ketogenic diet which is a low-carb diet has been popularly used since then.

It is high fat (70-80%), moderate protein (15-20%) and low carb diet.

The ketogenic diet aims to drive the body into a ketosis state where all the body's carb reservoir are depleted. Ketosis is beneficial to health and might help to prevent some chronic diseases.

Ketogenic foods are:

1. Animal protein such as fish, beef, eggs, poultry and organ meat.

2. Low-carb vegetables with no starch

3. Zero sugar, flour or refined food.

4. Little or no fruits. Only fruit with low sugar content like berries is permitted.

5. Fats in the form of butter, nut, healthy oils, and avocado.

Mediterranean Diet

The popular Mediterranean diet is based on the lifestyle of people in the Mediterranean countries (Spain, France, Italy) between 1940 and 1950. Although there is a slight variation in the actual diet. According to research, the menu is made up of 50% carbs, 30% fats, and 29% protein.

Mediterranean foods include:

1. Beans and legumes like lentils and peas

2. Rich fruits and vegetables

3. While grains like quinoa, brown rice

4. Reduced amount of meat products.

5. Little or no processed foods, flour or sugar.

6. Moderate wine drinking

7. A dairy product such as cheese and yogurt.

8. Fish as the primary source of protein for non-vegetarians

After it was discovered that this diet reduces the risk of chronic diseases including heart diseases, this diet became a favorable recommendation. These benefits are attributed to the oleic acid contained in olive oil and polyphenols in red wine.

Similarities between the Ketogenic Diet and Mediterranean Diet

1. Sodium Consumption

They both promote sodium intake. Mediterranean diet is rich in salt as a result of the oily dressings with increased amounts of salt and foods like cheese, olives, and anchovies. Keto diet encourages the addition of additional salts to maintain electrolytes balance since the meals are low in salt.

2. Healthy food

They both promote the consumption of protein and fresh vegetables and do not permit the use of chemicals, sugars, processed foods or additives.

3. Health benefits

There are many health benefits. Keto diet reduces the levels of total and LDL cholesterol, reduces the levels of triglycerides and increases the levels of HDL cholesterol which could be beneficial for people with type 2 diabetes and in fighting some cancers. Mediterranean diet advocates the use of olive oil which has been discovered to reduce the risk of heart disease, death, and stroke.

Differences between the Ketogenic and Mediterranean diet

These include:

Fat Consumption

Mediterranean diet has a lower fat percentage than the ketogenic diet. Mediterranean diet also advocates the use if unsaturated like gotten from fish and oils whereas keto foods include both saturated and in saturated oils.

Carbohydrate consumption.

The Mediterranean diet advocates high carb, healthy fats, and no refined sugars whereas the ketogenic diet restricts carbs in every form.

The Ketogenic Mediterranean diet involves 5-10% of alcohol, 7-10% of carbohydrates, 55-65% of fat and 22-30% of protein.

Foods include:

1. Non-starchy vegetables and plenty of salads.

2. Plenty healthy oils such as olive oil

3. Moderate wine drinking

4. Major protein source from fatty fish, lean meat, cheese and eggs

Similar to the ketogenic diet, there is a total restriction of sugars, flours, and starch. The only difference is that the fat source is different from the ketogenic diet and red wine is permitted.

Conclusion

They are both beneficial to health. It is advisable to start with the Mediterranean diet before moving to the ketogenic diet.

The Mediterranean Ketogenic Diet.

Ever wondered what diet plan would be created form blending the mysterious Mediterranean diet with a structured ketogenic diet? This is where the Mediterranean ketogenic diet comes in. The critical components of this diet include olive oil, red wine, fish and salad.

A few of the critical points of a structure ketogenic diet are:

1. Main protein source was fish.

2. Every day, the subject was asked to drink moderate amounts of wine.

3. Carbs were gotten mainly from salads and green vegetables.

4. Unrestricted calories- eating foods rich in fats creates a feeling of satiety, and this helps to suppress hunger.

Research Subjects of the Mediterranean Ketogenic Diets

This 12-week study was conducted with 40 obese subjects with an average Body Mass Index of 37; it was based on replacing their regular diet that promotes diabetes to a diet 50% rich in carbohydrates. The research was successful.

Ketone blood strips were used to confirm ketone levels each morning. I am afraid I have to disagree with this because if it ketone urine strike were used instead, the result would be incorrect after 2 or 3 weeks.

Results of this study include

1. These subjects had their weight reduced to 208 pounds, from an initial 240 pounds.

2. Evident fat loss in place of muscle loss

3. Reduction in blood pressure

4. Improvement in blood lipids.

5. Increase in HDL cholesterol

6. Reduction in blood glucose levels by about 29mg/dl

7. Reduction in levels of triglycerides which in turn reduces the risks of cancer, stroke and heart disease.

Seven Key Principles of the Mediterranean Ketogenic Diet

1. For many times, skip meals, eat heavy meals followed by periods of no meals.

Although heavy meals provide the nutrients that are essential for maximum functioning while also ensuring that our weight is healthy, it is not advisable to eat them throughout the day. Try not to snack. In actual Mediterranean diets, the Greeks are known to fast for about three months, this is responsible for the benefits of enhanced mental function, and improved heart function.

2. Green, Leafy vegetables

It is essential to include green leafy vegetables or cruciferous vegetables in each meal. They contain chemicals that improve immunity and fight cancer. Although the amount to be consumed depends on each person.

3. Instead of sweet foods, eat bitter foods

Similar to cruciferous and green vegetables, bitter foods like onions, bitter vegetables, bitter red wine, herbs, and garlic are rich in chemicals that improve the body's immunity. They prevent your taste buds from getting addicted to sweet and potentially unhealthy foods. Bitter foods also aid detoxification.

4. Minimize the quantity

Most effective diets involve some form of carbohydrate restriction to lower blood glucose and suppress insulin while helping the body to eliminate toxins. Although there is no standard value, nutritional ketosis needs less than 20 to 25 grams each day while very low or low carb diet is between 0 to 150 grams each day. Sources of carbohydrates can include sweet potato, blackberries, and yucca. They are usually optimized faster after exercising.

5. Consume large amounts of fat

A strict intermittent ketogenic diet is based on ample quantities of fat. The monounsaturated oil used in the Mediterranean diet is a good idea. Use rich cream, palm oil, macadamia, avocado and coconut oil with particularly for dressing, and with moderation.

6. Engage in routine exercises.

Engage in periods of exercises including resistance training and heavy weight lifting

It is important to know that the people of the Mediterranean engage in important routine exercise. They frequently take walks, engage in heavy lifting. Muscle contraction produces chemical substances that fight against cancer and inflammation.

7. 3 Rs: Relaxation, Recovery and Rest

In a society that is always on the go, we restrict the definition is a healthy lifestyle to only good and productivity.

We still require enough rest in various firms like sleep that enhances metabolism, regulate levels of blood glucose and boost immunity. You can engage your mind and also relax by socializing and reading. Other activities like gardening might require the use of your mind.

The mind, just like the body, needs to be rejuvenated.

These seven fundamental principles have been beneficial to me in maintaining a healthy lifestyle and weight. It has also helped to nourish my mind and body.

While on vacation recently, a few intense physical activities showed how I have unconsciously followed these principles. I recall my grandfather following similar principles. Although, part of his diet might not align with the principles of a Mediterranean ketogenic lifestyle there are quite some similarities.

Chapter 2 About the Fats: Extra Virgin Olive Oil

Reasons to Prove That Extra Virgin Olive Oil is The Healthiest Oil in Existence

Many controversies are surrounding the inclusion of fat in the diet.

It is common for people to argue about seed oils, animal fats and almost any type of fat.

However, out of all these fats, extra virgin olive oil is one fat that many people seem to agree on.

A staple in the Mediterranean diet, olive oil is a traditional fat that has been regularly included in the diets of some of the healthiest populations in the world.

Also, some studies have been conducted on the benefits of olive oil on health.

The researchers discovered that the antioxidants and fatty acids contained in olive oil are responsible for its significant benefits on the health, like lowering the risk of heart disease.

Olive oil- Definition and Production Processes

Olive oil is extracted from olives, the fruit produced by olive trees

The procedure is a straightforward one, the olives are pressed, and the olive starts to drop

Although there is a significant issue with olive oil, its appearance can be deceptive. Poor quality olive oils can be gotten with the use of chemicals or even mixing with other less expensive oils.

This, it is essential to buy authentic olive oil

The most authentic type is the extra virgin olive oil. It is processed naturally and checked for impurities and some sensory properties like smell and taste.

Genuine extra virgin olive oil has a peculiar taste and is rich in phenolic antioxidants, and this is the primary ingredient that is responsible for the benefits derived from natural olive oil.

Also, some olive oils are healthy, processed or 'thin,' they are gotten by using solvents, or heat, cheap oils such as canola and soybean oils have been used to dilute some of them.

This is the reason why extra virgin olive oil is the only type I would suggest.

Nutrient contained in extra virgin olive oil

Extra virgin olive oil is moderately nourishing.

Moderate quantities of Vitamin K and E and a lot of critical fatty acids are contained in olive oil.

The nutritional composition of 100g of olive oil is:

Vitamin E: 75% of RDA

Omega-3: 0.76% of RDA

Vitamin K: 75% of RDA

Saturated fat: 13.8% of RDA

Omega-6: 9.7% of RDA

Monounsaturated fat: 73% of RDA (almost entirely oleic acid)

However, the primary benefit of extra virgin olive oil is in the composition of antioxidants

Antioxidants are organic compounds that help prevent diseases

The vital antioxidants it contains includes oleuropein which prevents the oxidation of LDL Cholesterol and oleocanthal which is a potent anti-inflammatory compound.

Anti-Inflammatory compounds are contained in Extra Virgin Olive Oil

It is a widespread belief that most diseases are due to chronic inflammation; including cancer, diabetes, arthritis, metabolic syndromes, Alzheimer's, and heart disease.

Some hypothesis suggests that the anti-inflammatory properties of olive oil are responsible for the majority of its benefits.

Evidence suggests that the primary fatty acid contained in olive oil- oleic acid can help to lower inflammatory substances like C-Reactive Protein

Although, the significant anti-inflammatory properties is due to the antioxidants contained in olive oil, especially oleocanthal which has been discovered to produce effects similar to ibuprofen, a widely used anti-inflammatory drug.

Various studies have estimated that the quantity of oleocanthal in 3 to 4 tablespoons (around 50mls) of extra virgin olive oil works in the same way as 10% of the dosage of ibuprofen in an adult to relieve pain.

Another research also discovered that compound present in olive oil could suppress the proteins and genes that promote inflammation.

Remember that chronic, low-level inflammation usually is mild and the damage is done after many years or decades.

Extra Virgin Olive Oil Protects Against Diseases of the Cardiovascular System

Diseases of the cardiovascular system such as stroke or heart disease are the most popular causes of death worldwide.

Many researchers have discovered that death resulting from these diseases is low in specific areas such as the countries at the border of the Mediterranean Sea.

This research made people curious about the Mediterranean Diet, that is presumed to imitate the eating habits of people in those countries.

Researches on the Mediterranean diet have discovered that it can help to fight against heart disease. According to one significant study, it lowered strokes, death and heart attacks by 30%

These are some of the mechanisms with which Extra Virgin olive oil prevents heart diseases

Reduces inflammation: As stated previously, olive oil is anti-inflammatory; inflammation is responsible for most heart diseases.

LDL cholesterol: Olive oil prevents the oxidation of LDL cholesterol which is a significant process in the development of heart disease

Enhances the functions of the endothelium: The endothelium is the inner layer of blood vessels, olive oil improves endothelial function.

Olive oil and cancer

One major cause of death is cancer. Cancer is caused by the unlimited growth of the body's cells.

Research has discovered that people in the Mediterranean have a moderately reduced risk of cancer and there have been some theories that suggest that it might be due to olive oil.

A significant cause of cancer is oxidative damage caused by free radicals; however, extra virgin olive oil is rich in antioxidants that can prevent oxidative damage.

The oleic acid present in olive oil prevents oxidation and have been discovered to be beneficial in protecting against cancer-promoting genes.

Some in-vitro research has discovered that some substances in olive oil can fight against cancer at the level of molecules.

Although, there have been no human trials to prove that olive oil can prevent cancer.

Olive oil and Alzheimer's Disease

The most common neurodegenerative disease in the world is Alzheimer's disease, which is also a significant cause of dementia

Alzheimer's disease is caused by the accumulation of protein products known as beta-amyloid plaques in specific neurons in the brain.

One trial involving humans discovered that a Mediterranean diet rich in olive oil has beneficial effects on the functions of the brain and lowers the risks associated with mental deterioration.

Can It be Uses To Prepare Your Meals?

Cooking can cause the oxidation of fatty acids. This means that they react with oxygen and are destroyed.

This is mainly due to the double bonds in the fatty acid molecules.

Because of this, saturated fats(without double bonds) are not easily destroyed by increased temperature; whereas, polyunsaturated fats (a lot of double bonds) are susceptible and are destroyed.

Olive oil which is rich in monounsaturated fatty acids (just one double bond) is not easily destroyed by high heat.

One research involved heating extra virgin love oil at a temperature of 356 degrees Fahrenheit (180 degrees Celsius) for a period of 36 hours. The olive oil was not destroyed easily.

Another research deep-fried with olive oil and harmful levels were only reached after about 24-27 hours.

To sum this up, olive oil is not harmful even when cooking at moderately high temperatures.

Conclusion

The health benefits of olive oil are tremendous.

Olive oil is indeed great for people with heart disease or high-risk individuals.

Although, it is imperative to buy the authentic type, which is undiluted extra virgin olive oils.

Contrary to what we see most times, many people agree that this oil is genuinely beneficial.

Chapter 3 The Keto Mediterranean Diet Recipes

Almond berry Muffins

Servings: 12

Preparation Time: 35 minutes

Ingredients

- 2 Tbs of avocado oil
- 2 1/2 cup of almond flour
- pinch of salt
- 1/3 cup of granulated stevia sweetener
- 2 tsp of baking powder
- 1/3 cup of fresh butter softened
- 1/3 cup of almond milk unsweetened
- 1 tsp pure almond extract
- 3 eggs from free-range chickens
- 2/3 cup of fresh berries (blueberries, raspberries, strawberries...)
- Zest of 1/2 lemon

Instructions

1. Preheat oven to 350° F/175° C.

2. Line a 12 -cup muffin pan with muffin liners.

3. Grease each cup with avocado oil.

4. In a bowl, combine almond flour, stevia sweetener, pinch of salt and baking powder.

5. Add in butter, almond milk, almond extract, eggs and lemon zest.

6. Stir lightly with a cooking whisk until combine.

7. Add berry mixture and gently stir to combine well.

8. Scoop butter into each cup cake, about 3/4 of the way full.

9. Bake for about 25 minutes.

10. Let cool, remove muffins from cupcakes and serve.

11. Place muffins in a bag, close and seal and keep at room temperature up to 3 days or refrigerate or freeze them.

Marinated Mushrooms in Apple Cider

Servings: 6

Preparation Time: 20 minutes

Ingredients

- 3 lbs fresh white mushrooms
- 2 cups apple cider vinegar (preferably non-pasteurized)
- 6 cloves   garlic, chopped
- 1/2 tsp salt   to taste

Instructions

1. In a saucepan place mushrooms, garlic, salt and vinegar.

2. Blanch mushrooms in distilled vinegar bringing to boil.

3. Remove from heat and let cool completely.

4. Store marinated mushrooms in the refrigerator.

Macadamia Breaded Tuna Patties

Servings: 6

Preparation Time: 15 minutes

Ingredients

- 2 can (15 oz) tuna in oil, drained
- 1/2 cup ground Macadamia nuts
- 1 tsp of fresh thyme, chopped
- 3 large free-range eggs
- 1 Lemon zest
- 1/4 cup sunflower oil for frying

Instructions

1. Drain the tuna, place in a bowl, and mix it with the fork.

2. Place all remaining ingredients from the list above.

3. Stir well, and then shape small burgers.

4. Roll each burger in ground macadamia.

5. Fry tuna burgers 3 - 4 minutes per side (for medium-rare) or until get a golden brown color outside.

6. Remove from the pan, and let rest for 5 minutes.

7. Serve hot or warm.

Slow Cooked Beef and Broccoli

Servings: 4

Preparation Time: 4 hours and 10 minutes

Ingredients

- 1 Tbs of tallow softened
- 1 1/2 lbs skirt steak (cuts from the round) cut into cubes
- Salt and ground pepper to taste
- 1 cup of bone broth
- 1 cup of Coconut aminos
- 1 Tbs of granulated stevia sweetener
- 1 Tbs of apple cider vinegar
- 3/4 tsp of red pepper flake
- 2 cloves of garlic finely sliced
- 2 heads of broccoli

Instructions

1. Grease your Slow Cooker with softened tallow.

2. Add the beef on the bottom and sprinkle with the salt and pepper.

3. In a bowl, combine the bone broth, Coconut aminos, stevia sweetener, vinegar and the red pepper flakes.

4. Pour the mixture over the beef and cover.

5. Cook on HIGH for 2 hours.

6. Open and add broccoli and finely sliced garlic.

7. Cover lid and cook on LOW for another 2 hours or until broccoli is tender.

8. Serve hot or warm.

Baked Cauliflower "Pastry" with Bacon

Servings: 6

Preparation Time: 50 minutes

Ingredients

- 2 Tbs of olive oil
- 1 large head cauliflower grated
- 8 large eggs from free-range chicken
- 1 cup of almond milk
- 2 cloves garlic finely chopped
- 2 tsp of sweet paprika
- Salt and ground black pepper
- 1 1/2 cups of Parmesan cheese grated
- 2 green onions finely sliced
- 6 slices bacon cut into cubes

Instructions

1. Preheat oven to 350F/180C.

2. Grease the large baking dish with olive oil.

3. Winse, pat dry and grate cauliflower with grater.

4. Add grated cauliflower into prepared baking dish.

5. Sprinkle cauliflower with grated parmesan, bacon cubes, and green onions

6. In a bowl, whisk together eggs, almond milk, chopped garlic, salt and pepper, and sweet paprika.

7. Pour the egg mixture evenly into baking dish.

8. Bake for 35 to 40 minutes.

9. Serve hot or warm.

Oven Baked Chicken With Olives

Servings: 4

Preparation Time: 50 minutes

Ingredients

- 1/4 cup garlic-infuse olive oil
- 1 1/2 lb   chicken breast boneless and skinless
- 1 bunch fresh thyme sprigs
- salt and freshly ground black pepper
- 1 spring onion (only green parts), finely chopped
- 1 cup olives (green and black), pitted
- zest of 1 lemon
- 1 cup fresh lemon juice

Instructions

1. Spread thyme evenly in the bottom of baking dish.

2. Place the chicken over thyme sprigs. Season the salt and pepper.

3. Whisk chopped spring onion, olives, olive oil, lemon zest, lemon juice, pinch of salt and ground pepper in a bowl.

4. Pour the mixture over chicken.

5. Cover and refrigerate for at least 2-3 hours.

6. Preheat oven to 400F/200C.

7. Remove chicken from the fridge and   bake until cooked through, 35-40 minutes (an internal temperature has to be 165°F).

8. Serve hot or warm.

Famous Radicchio Tardivo di Treviso

Cooking Time: 18 minutes

Ingredients

- 5 thick heads of radicchio tardivo di treviso
- Salt and freshly ground black pepper
- ½ cup of extra-virgin olive oil

Instructions

1. Preheat oven to 400 F/200 C.

2. Discard any wilted outer leaves from radicchio heads and cut off discolored stem ends.

3. Rinse under cold running water and shake off moisture.

4. Cut each head of radicchio in half lengthwise, then make a V-cut in the root end, cutting half as deep as the root is thick and running the cut from the bottom to the point where the leaves join the root.

5. Arrange radicchio halves cut side up in a baking pan, overlapping if necessary.

6. Season generously with salt and pepper and drizzle with 4 tablespoon of the oil.

7. Bake for about 12 minutes, then turn radicchio over.

8. Bake for another 8 minutes, then turn radicchio again so that the cut side is facing up.

9. Drizzle with remaining 2 tablespoon of oil if necessary, and bake until the root end is tender when pierced with a knife, about 2 minutes more.

10. Serve hot or warm.

Broiled Sea Bass with Fresh Herbs

Servings: 4

Total Time: 25 minutes

Ingredients

- 2 Tbs extra virgin olive oil
- 1 tsp fresh thyme chopped
- 1 tsp dried lavender
- 1/2 Tbs fresh basil chopped
- 1 tsp   garlic, finely chopped
- 1/2 tsp sea salt (or to taste)
- 1/4 tsp grated black pepper (or to taste)
- 4 fillets Sea bass without skin sea
- Lemon slices for serving (optional)
- Olive oil for greasing

Instructions

1. Preheat the oven to 400F/200C.

2. Grease with olive oil a shallow glass or ceramic baking dish.

3. Trim each sea bass fillet and remove the skin.

4. In a small bowl, combine together a thyme, lavender, basil, garlic, salt and pepper and stir well.

5. Apply herb   mixture and rub on both sides of   fish fillets.

6. Place the fish fillets in prepared baking dish.

7. Bake uncovered for 20 minutes or until the thickest part of the fish flakes easily).

8. Serve warm and garnish with lemon slices.

Baked Shrimps with Sun-dried Tomatoes

Servings: 4

Preparation Time: 55 minutes

Ingredients

- 20 large shrimps, cleaned, fresh or frozen
- 1/4 cup lemon juice
- 2/3 cup garlic infused olive oil
- 1 spring onion (only green parts)
- 4 sun-dried tomatoes, preserved in oil
- 1 tsp sweet paprika
- 1 red chilli pepper
- 1 cup fresh tomato juice
- Salt and ground pepper to taste

Instructions

1. Clean, wash and drain the shrimp.

2. Put the shrimps in a bowl, squeeze half a lemon, and add peppers and pinch of salt; stir.

3. Cover with a plastic cover and marinate in fridge for one hour.

4. Heat half the oil in a frying skillet over medium heat.

5.Sauté spring onion, sun-dried tomatoes, salt and pepper   until soft.

6.Then, add   tomato juice and sweet pepper and chili pepper and let it boil for 5 minutes; stir.

7.Preheat oven to 360F.

8.Remove the shrimp from the refrigerator and place in baking dish.

9.Pour the sauce over the shrimps and add salt, freshly ground pepper and pour the remaining oil.

10. Bake in the oven for 30-40 minutes or until golden brown.

11. Serve hot or warm..

Baked Walnut Croissant Cookies

Servings: 12

Preparation Time: 35 minutes

Ingredients

- 1/3 lb of grated walnuts
- 1/3 lb of fresh butter at room temperature
- 2 1/4 cups powdered stevia sweetener
- 1/3 lb of almond flour
- 1 tsp of baking powder

Instructions

1. Preheat oven to 320 F/160 C.

2. Mix butter with stevia sweetener in the stand mixer with the dough hook.

3. Add grated walnuts, almond flour and baking powder.

4. Beat until the dough starts separating from the bowl.

5. Fill up half the each Croissant Silicone Molds.

6. Gently sprinkle with chopped walnuts. and bake for 10 - 12 minutes.

Bell Peppers Stuffed with Minced Meat

Servings: 6

Preparation Time: 40 minutes

Ingredients

- 6 large green bell peppers
- 2 Tbsp olive oil
- 2 scallion (only green parts) finely chopped
- 1 1/2 lb minced meat (beef or chicken)
- 1/2 cup grated tomatoes
- 2 carrot, grated
- 1 1/2 Tbs Worcestershire Sauce
- 3/4 cup   feta cheese, crumbled
- 1 Tbs fresh parsley, finely chopped
- salt and ground black pepper to taste
- 3/4 cup water

Instructions

1. Preheat the oven to 380F/190C. Grease a baking pan; set aside.

2. Rinse and cut the top of each pepper; clean spores and membranes.

3. Heat the oil in a large frying pan over medium heat.

4.Sauté the green parts of scallion with pinch of salt until soft, about 4 - 5 minutes.

5.Reduce the heat to medium, and add the minced meat. Cook about 5 minutes stirring frequently.

6.Add the grated tomato, carrots and Worcestershire sauce; give a good stir.

7.Remove from heat and let it rest for 10 minutes.

8.Add chopped parsley and stir again.

9.Fill the peppers with ground meat mixture, and place them on prepared baking pan.

10.Sprinkle with crumbled Feta.

11. Pour water evenly and place the pan in your oven.

12. Bake for 20 minutes.

13. Serve hot or warm..

Spicy Broccoli with Garlic Stew

Servings: 2

Preparation Time: 20 minutes

Ingredients

- 1 cup extra-virgin olive oil
- 1 lb of broccoli, stemmed and cut into florets
- 3 cloves garlic, finely chopped
- 1 tsp crushed red chile flakes
- Water, Kosher salt, to taste

Instructions

1. Heat oil in a frying skillet over medium-high heat.

2. Add broccoli; cook, turning occasionally, until lightly browned, 6–8 minutes.

3. Sprinkle   water; add garlic, and cook until golden, 2–3 minutes.

4. Add crushed red chile flakes; cook until toasted, about 2 minutes.

5. Season with salt.

Breaded Anchovies with Thistle and Cumin

Servings: 6

Cooking Times: 15 minutes

Ingredients

- 2 lbs of anchovies cleaned
- 3/4 cup of almond flour
- Sea salt and ground pepper to taste
- 1 tsp of cumin
- 1 tsp of garlic powder
- 1 tsp of dry thistle spice (or substitute with parsley)
- Extra virgin olive oil for frying
- Lemon wedges for servings

Instructions

1. Rinse well the anchovies and place on a kitchen paper towel to dry.

2. In a large bowl, combine the almond flour, salt and pepper, cumin, garlic powder and thistle spice.

3. Roll anchovies in a flour mixtures.

4. Heat the olive oil in a large frying skillet at medium-high heat.

5. Fry the fish only for 2 - 3 minutes   or until golden brown.

6. Remove the fish on a on a kitchen paper towel.

7. Serve with the lemon wedges.

Broccoli Chowder with Ground Meat

Servings: 6

Cooking Times

Preparation Time: 40 minutes

Instructions

- 3 Tbs of butter
- 2 cloves of garlic
- 3/4 lb of ground beef (from chuck steak)
- 1 medium head of broccoli cut into flower clusters
- 1 tomato grated
- 1 Tbs of fresh parsley finely chopped
- 1 cup of bone broth
- 1 cup of water
- 1 tsp of cumin, cayenne pepper and ground paprika mixture
- salt to taste
- 2 Tbs of canned coconut milk for serving (optional)

Instructions

1. Heat the butter in a large pot over medium heat.

2. Sauté the garlic with the pinch of salt until soft.

3. Add ground meat, stir and cook for 2 to 3 minutes.

4. Add all remaining ingredients, stir well, cover and simmer on a medium-low heat for 30 minutes.

5. Taste and adjust salt to taste; give a good stir.

6. Serve hot with a coconut milk.

Calamari with Chorizo and Artichokes

Servings: 4

Cooking Times: 25 minutes

Ingrdients

- 1/3 cup of olive oil
- 4 oz cured Spanish chorizo, peeled and thinly sliced
- 4 cloves garlic, thinly sliced
- 4 whole calamari, cleaned, tentacles reserved
- Kosher salt and freshly ground black pepper, to taste
- 2 cups artichoke hearts, defrosted frozen quarters or whole canned, drained and halved
- 1 orange, zested, supremed, and cut into 1" pieces

Instructions

1. Heat oil in a large frying skillet over medium-high heat.

2. Add chorizo and garlic; cook until golden, 3-4 minutes.

3. Divide mixture between 4 plates; keep warm.

4. Add some more oil to the frying skillet and increase to medium-high heat.

5. Pat dry calamari and tentacles using kitchen paper towels, and season with salt and pepper.

6. Cook, flipping once, until browned and slightly curled, 4-6 minutes; divide between plates.

7. Add artichokes, salt, and pepper to pan; cook until browned, 3-4 minutes, and divide between plates.

8. Garnish with chopped orange and zest.

Oven Baked Scallops with Parmesan

Servings: 8

Preparation Time: 15 minutes

Ingredients

- 8 diver scallops
- 8 scallop shells
- 4 Tbs grated Parmesan
- 1 1/2 Tbs of ground almonds or almond flour
- 2 Tbsp of olive oil
- 3 sprigs thyme, stemmed
- Kosher salt and freshly ground black pepper, to taste

Instructions

1. Heat broiler to high.

2. Put scallops in shells; place on baking sheet.

3. Stir together Parmesan, ground almonds, oil, thyme, and salt and pepper; and divide among scallops.

4. Broil until browned, about 3 minutes.

Braised Artichoke Hearts with Mint

Servings: 6

Preparation Time: 35 minutes

Ingredients

- 6 large trimmed artichoke hearts with stems
- 2 cups white wine
- 1 cup extra-virgin olive oil
- 3 Tbs minced fresh flat-leaf parsley
- 3 Tbs minced mint leaves
- 2 Tbs fresh lemon juice
- 4 cloves garlic, minced
- Kosher salt and freshly ground black pepper, to taste

Instructions

1. Place artichokes in a large saucepan along with wine, oil, parsley, mint, lemon juice, garlic, and 2 cups water.

2. Season with the salt and pepper and bring to a boil.

3. Reduce heat to medium-low and simmer artichokes, turning occasionally, until tender, 15–20 minutes.

4. Transfer artichokes stem side up to a platter and drizzle with some of the cooking liquid.

Simple Roasted Artichokes Appetizer

Servings: 8

Preparation Time: 1 hour and 20 minutes

Ingredients

- 1 cup of olive oil
- 1 cup of dry white wine
- 2 Tbsp of dried oregano
- 2–3 tsp crushed red chile flakes
- 8 cloves garlic, finely chopped
- Kosher salt and freshly ground black pepper, to taste
- 6 artichokes, stemmed

Instructions

1. Heat oven to 450 F/225C.

2. In a bowl, whisk together oil, wine, oregano, chile flakes, garlic, and salt and pepper; set aside.

3. Cut 1" off top of each artichoke and gently pull leaves apart to open artichokes.

4. Place them, standing up on their bases, in a small roasting pan or dish large enough to hold them in one layer.

5. Pour oil mixture over each artichoke.

6. Cover with aluminum foil, and bake for 45 minutes.

7. Uncover, and bake, basting often with juices, until browned and tender, about 30 minutes more.

8. Let cool for 10 minutes before serving.

Chicken and Cabbage-Carrot Hash

Servings: 6

Preparation Time: 50 minutes

Ingredients

- 2 chicken breast halves, boneless and skinless
- 6 cups water
- 2 leeks, finely chopped, bulb and lower leaf portion
- 4 carrots, sliced
- 1/2 head green cabbage, shredded
- Salt and black ground pepper
- Tarragon, caraway and thyme to taste

Instructions

1. Seasone the chicken breasts with salt and add with water to a Dutch oven.

2. Bring to a boil and let simmer for about 20 minutes, or until chicken is cooked through.

3. Remove the chicken from the broth and set aside to cool.

4. Put the leeks and carrots into the pot and simmer for 10 minutes.

5. Shred the cooled chicken in to bite sized pieces and return it to the pot.

6. Add the cabbage and and cook for 8 - 10 minutes

7. Add herbs to taste, stir and cook for 2 minutes.

8. Taste and adjust salt and pepper.

9. Serve hot or warm..

Tuscany Chicken Cutlets with Seasoning

Servings: 6

Preparation Time: 20 minutes

Ingredients

- 6   chicken cutlets, boneless
- Salt and freshly ground black pepper to taste
- 2 Tbs olive oil
- 1 Tbsp Tuscany Italian Seasoning
- 1/4 cup fresh parsley, chopped
- 1 Tbsp   fresh chives, chopped
- 3 Tbs capers, rinsed and drained
- 2 Tbs fresh lemon juice; to taste
- 3/4 cup water

Instructions

1. Season the chicken cutlets with Italian Seasoning.

2. Heat the olive in a frying skillet over medium-high heat.

3. Add the chicken cutlets and sauté for about 4 minutes minutes.

4. Flip the chicken cutlets and sauté the other side for 2 - 3 minutes.

5. Add parsley, chives and capers and stir.

6. Pour the lemon juice and water and stir well.

7. Reduce heat and simmer it uncovered for 5 minutes.

8. Remove from heat and serve immediately.

Puntarelle in Salsa di Alici

Servings: 4

Cooking Time: 20 minutes

Ingredients

- 8 oz young dandelion greens, trimmed and thinly sliced
- 4 anchovy filets
- 1 clove garlic, minced
- 6 Tbs extra-virgin olive oil
- 3 Tbs red or white wine vinegar
- Kosher salt and freshly ground black pepper, to taste

Instructions

1. Put puntarelle into a bowl of ice water; let sit for 1 hour.

2. Meanwhile, finely chop and smash anchovies and garlic to make a paste; whisk in oil and vinegar to make a smooth dressing. Season with salt and pepper.

3. Drain puntarelle and pat dry; toss with dressing.

4. Serve.

Spiced Green Beans with Cinnamon

Servings: 6

Cooking Times: 1 hour and 5 minutes

Ingredients

- 2 Tbs garlic - infused olive oil
- 1 spring onion, finely chopped (only green parts)
- 2 lb fresh green beans - trimmed and cut diagonally in half
- 1 tsp red pepper flakes
- 2 tomatoes, coarsely chopped
- 1/2 cup water
- 1/2 tsp cinnamon
- salt and black pepper, freshly ground

Instructions

1. Heat the olive in a large pot over medium heat.

2. Sauté the green parts of   spring onions for 3 - 4 minutes with pinch of salt.

3. Add the red pepper flakes and chopped tomatoes; sauté for 5 minutes.

4. Add the green beans and give a good stir.

5. Pour water, cover lid and cook for 35   minutes until completely soft.

6. Add the cinnamon, salt, pepper and serve.

Creamy Chilly Cucumber Soup

Servings: 4

Cooking Time: 40 minutes

Ingredients

- FOR THE ICE CUBES:
- 3 Tbs mint leaves, cut into chiffonade
- 1 Tbs lemon juice
- Salt to taste
- FOR THE SOUP:
- 1 lb of cucumbers, peeled, diced
- 1 1/2   cup of plain Greek yogurt
- 1 cup lemon juice
- 1 cup of mint leaves
- 2 Tbsp of chives, roughly chopped
- 3 Tbsp of extra virgin olive oil
- Salt to taste

Instructions

1. Divide the mint, lemon juice, and salt among 4 cubes of an ice cube tray.

2. Top with cold water and freeze.

3. In a blender, combine the cucumber, yogurt, lemon juice, mint, chives, olive oil, and salt.

4. Blend until completely smooth.

5. Taste and adjust seasonings.

6. Pour soup into individual bowls and top each with a lemon-mint ice cube.

Scallops au Gratin Style with Grape Juice

Servings: 6

Ingredients

- 2 cups of grape juice
- 1 bay leaf
- 1 large shallot, quartered
- salt and freshly ground white pepper, to taste
- 18 medium sea scallops
- 1 cup of unsalted butter, softened
- 16 oz of button mushrooms, sliced
- 3 Tbs of flour
- 1 cup of heavy cream
- 1 tsp offresh lemon juice
- 1 ½ cups of grated Gruyere

Instructions

1. Boil grape juice, bay leaf, shallot, salt, white pepper, and 1 cup water in a large pot over medium heat.

2. Add scallops; cook until just tender, 1–2 minutes.

3. Divide scallops between six cleaned scallop shells or shallow gratin dishes.

4. Simmer cooking liquid until reduced to 3 cup, 5–7 minutes. Strain liquid; set aside.

5. In a separated frying skillet melt butter over medium-high heat.

6. Cook mushrooms with a pinch of salt until soft.

7. Divide mushrooms between scallop shells.

8. Stir in flour; cook 2 minutes.

9. Add reserved cooking liquid, the cream, lemon juice, salt, and white pepper; bring to a boil.

10. Cook until sauce is slightly thick, about 6 minutes.

11. Spoon sauce over scallops and top with Gruyere; broil until cheese is melted and golden, 2–3 minutes.

Bacon-Wrapped Artichokes

Servings: 6

Cooking Times: 20 minutes

Ingredients

- ½ cup of oil oil, for frying
- 30 oz canned artichoke hearts
- 8 slices bacon, halved crosswise
- 1/3 cup freshly grated Parmesan
- Salt and ground of black pepper

Instructions

1. Heat the oil in a large frying skillet over medium-high heat.

2. Place each artichoke heart on one end of a bacon slice, sprinkle with some of the Parmesan and pepper, and roll up; secure with a toothpick.

3. Fry bacon-wrapped artichokes until golden brown, about 3 minutes.

4. Drain and serve hot.

Crabmeat and Crumbled Eggs Hash

Servings: 6

Preparation Time: 45 minutes

Ingredients

- 4 large eggs from free-range chickens, hard boiled
- ¼ cup of olive oil
- 2 fresh onions finely sliced
- pinch of sea salt
- 4 radishes, finely sliced
- 15 oz of fresh or frozen crab meat
- 1 cup of fish broth
- 3 Tbs of fresh dill, chopped
- 3 cucumbers cut into cubes
- Mayonnaise to taste

Instructions

1. Boil eggs (12 minutes for hard boiled), cool and peel; set aside.

2. Heat the oil in a large frying skillet and sauté green onions with a pinch of salt.

3. Add radishes and fish broth, and simmer for 6 to 8   minutes over medium heat.

4. Stir in crab meat   and fresh dill; cook for 10 to 12 minutes.

5. Remove from the heat and add cucumber and sliced eggs.

6. Toss to combine well.

7. Serve with a mayonnaise.

Velvety Chicken and Broccoli Stew

Servings: 6

Preparation Time: 30 minutes

Ingredients

- 2 Tbs of chicken lard (non-hydrogenated)
- 1 lb chicken breast fillet, cut in small cubes
- 3 ½ oz of bacon, sliced
- 2 cloves of garlic finely chopped
- 1 scallion finely chopped
- ½ cup of cream cheese (or mascrapone)
- 4 Tbs of grated parmesan cheese
- 1 broccoli head cut into flowerets
- 1 cup of fresh cream
- 1 cup of chicken broth
- 1 cup of water
- 1 tsp of dried oregano
- salt and black pepper to taste

Instructions

1. Heat the chicken fat in a frying skillet over medium-high heat.

2. Sauté the chicken for 3 minutes from all sides.

3. Remove the chicken to the plate; set aside.

4. In the same skillet, sauté the garlic and the scallion with the pinch of salt.

5. Pour the broth, water and cream; stir well.

6. Bring to boil, and add the cream cheese (or mascrapone).

7. Stir until the cheeses are melted.

8. Add the broccoli flowerts, reduce heat and cook uncovered for 5 to 7 minutes.

45

9. Add the chicken cubes and season with the oregano, salt and pepper.

10. Cover and cook for 3 minutes.

11. In a separate skillet fry the bacon slices until crunchy.

12. Crumble bacon and add to the skillet.

13. Stir, adjust the salt and pepper and remove from heat.

14. Serve hot or warm.

Cretan Tomato Eggs Mash

Servings: 4

Preparation Time: 15 minutes

Ingredients

- 1/4 cup garlic-infused olive oil
- 4 spring onions (only green parts), chopped
- 4 large tomatoes finely chopped
- 8 Free-range eggs
- 1 tsp fresh basil (chopped)
- 1 tsp oregano
- salt and ground black pepper to taste

Instructions

1. Heat the olive oil in a frying skillet on medium-high heat.

2. Add scallions and with a pinch of saltm and sauté for 3 - 4   minutes until softened.

3. Whisk the eggs with basil, oregano, and the salt and pepper.

4. Pour the egg mixture to skillet over scallions and tomatoes.

5. Cook for 2   minutes; stir frequently.

6. Serve hot or warm.

Creamy Mascarpone Chicken Breasts

Servings: 4

Cooking Time: 25 minutes

Ingredients

- 2 chicken breasts, boneless
- 1/4 cup of olive oil
- 2 leeks, finely chopped, bulb and lower leaf portion
- 1 cup of almond milk
- 1 cup of Mascarpone cheese
- salt and pepper to taste
- ¼ cup of fresh parsley chopped

Instructions

1. Cut the chicken breasts into pieces.

2. Heat the oil in frying skillet over medium-strong heat.

3. Sauté the chicken breast from all sides for 3-4 minutes.

4. Remove the chicken from the skillet and set aside.

5. In the same pan, heat the olive oil, and sauté the leeks with pinch of salt for about 5 minutes.

6.Pour the almond milk and grated Mascarpone   cheese.

7.Stir and simmer over low heat until all ingredients combined well.

8.Add the chicken breasts, stir well, and cook over a low heat for 10 minutes; stir to avoid sticking.

9.Sprinkle with parsley and serve hot.

Stringig Nettle Soup with Feta Cheese

Servings: 6

Preparation Time: 25 minutes

Ingredients

- 1 1/2 lbs. bunch of nettles
- 4 green onion (only green parts finely chopped)
- ¼ cup garlic-infused olive oil
- 3 cups of water
- 3 cups of vegetable broth
- 1 cup Feta cheese crumbled
- Salt and pepper to taste

Instructions

1. Carefully cut the stems of nettles, and wash in water.

2. Cut nettles and with the sharp knife.

3. Pour the oil to the inner stainless steel pot in the Instant Pot.

4. Add all ingredients (except Feta) in your Instant Pot.

5. Lock lid into place and set on the SOUP/STEW setting for 6 minutes.

6. Use the Quick Release and allow valve to let the pressure out.

7. Transfer the soup in your blender and add crumbled Feta cheese.

8. Blend until smooth and creamy.

9. Taste and adjust salt and pepper to taste.

10. Serve hot or warm.

Delicious Shrimp with Anis and Saffron

Servings: 4, Cooking Times: 35 minutes

Ingredients

- 3/4 cup of olive oil
- 28 medium shrimps, cleaned
- 2 green onions finely chopped
- 1 Tbsp of vodka
- 1/2 tsp of ground anis
- 2 small tomatoes, pealed and grated
- 1/2 Tbs of saffron threads
- 4 Tbs of cream cheese (full fat)
- salt and freshly ground pepper

Instructions

1. Heat 4 tablespoon of olive oil in a pot, and sauté the onions and shrimps; season with the salt and pepper.

2. Season shrimp with salt and pepper, and when they change color and become pink, add water to cover them.

3. Cover lid and cook for 20 minutes.

4. Remove the pot from the heat; discard the broth (reserve) and place the shrimp on a plate.

5. Sprinkle the shrimp with the saffron threads.

6. Heat the remaining oil and add the shrimp; saute for 1 - 2 minutes.

7. Pour vodka, add anis, grated tomato, 1 cup of reserved broth, and the salt and pepper.

8. Cook for 4 - 5 minute; stir gently.

9. Finally, stir the cream cheese and stir for further 2 - 3 minutes.

10. Serve hot or warm.

Traditional Greek Tzatziki Salad

Servings: 8

Preparation Time: 15 minutes

Ingredients

- Kosher or sea salt
- 4 medium cloves garlic
- 1-1/2 cups plain Greek yogurt
- 3/4 cup finely chopped cucumber, peeled
- 1 Tbsp of red-wine vinegar
- 2 tsp   of fresh mint, chopped
- 2 tsp of fresh dill, chopped
- 2 Tbsp of garlic-infused olive oil
- Fresh mint leaves for garnish (optional)

Instructions

1. Spread 3/4 teaspoon of salt on a cutting board.

2. Peel garlic and finely chop it.

3. Transfer garlic and salt to a medium bowl and stir the yogurt.

4. Put the cucumber in a colander and drain.

5. Add the cucumber, vinegar, mint, dill, and olive oil to the yogurt mixture.

6. Stir to blend and season with the salt to taste.

7. Cover and chill for at least 4 hours before serving.

8. Serve cool, garnished with chopped mint leaves.

9. Keep in a covered container in refrigerator.

Delicious Baked Fishburgers

Servings: 3

Cooking Times: 25 minutes

Ingredients

- 1 1/2 lbs fish (sea bream, hammer, etc.) ground or finely chopped
- 1/4 cup of olive oil
- 1 cup of green onions, finely chopped
- 3 cloves of garlic, finely chopped
- 1 Tbs of fresh ginger, finely chopped
- 1/2 cup of ground almonds
- 1 pasturased egg
- 1/2 tsp of fresh chopped mint
- 1 tsp lemon zest
- 1/2 tsp of dry coriander
- Salt to taste

Instructions

1. Heat 2   tablespoon of oil in a frying pan over medium-high   heat.

2. Sauté the onions and garlic with a pinch of salt until soft.

3. Add the garlic and ginger and sauté for 2 minutes.

4. Remove the mixture from the heat and allow to cool well.

5. Combine the onion mixture with all remaining ingredients and knead well.

6. With your hands shape the fish burgers.

7. Heat the oil in a non-stick frying skillet over high heat, and fry the burgers until they get good color from both sides.

Frying Sesame Quails

Servings: 4

Cooking Times: 30 minutes

Ingredients

- 4 big quail
- 2 Tbs fresh butter grass fed
- 2 tsp sesame seeds
- 2 Tbs white wine vinegar
- 1/4 cup garlic-infused oil
- Salt and freshly ground pepper

Instructions

1. Season quails with the salt and pepper.

2. Heat the butter in a deep frying pan over medium heat; sauté quails just to take color.

3. Cover and let cook for another 10 minutes over medium heat.

4. In a bowl, stir the vinegar, oil, salt and pepper and sesame seeds.

5. Pour the vinegar dressing over the quails; toss to combine well.

6. Heat the remaining oil in a frying skillet and fry the quails for 10   minutes from all sides.

8. Serve hot or warm.

Stuffed Zucchini with Anchovies

Ingredients

- 4 Tbsp of olive oil
- 24 canned anchovies
- 24 slices of zucchini blossoms, stamens discarded
- 1 cup of all-purpose flour
- 2 Tbs baking powder
- Salt and freshly ground black pepper, to taste
- 1 ½ cup of beer

Instructions

1. Heat oil in a large frying skillet.

2. Place 1 anchovy fillet in each zucchini blossom and roll lengthwise to wrap.

3. Whisk flour, baking powder, salt, and pepper in a bowl; whisk in beer until batter forms.

4. Dip zucchini blossoms in batter; fry until golden and crisp, 1–2 minutes.

5. Drain on a kitchen paper towels.

6. Season with the salt and pepper to taste and serve.

Artichoke Hearts with Sesame Seed Paste

Servings: 6, Cooking Times: 25 minutes

Ingredients

- For the sauce:
- 6 cloves of garlic, finely chopped
- 2 tsp of salt
- 1 cup of sesame seed paste
- 1 cup fresh lemon juice
- 2 to 3 Tbsp of water
- 3 tsp chopped fresh parsley
- For artichokes:
- 2 cups of olive oil
- 8 hearts of steamed medium artichokes
- 1 cup of flour
- 1 pinch of salt

Instructions

1. Combine finely chopped garlic with sesame seed paste.

2. Drizzle in lemon juice; stire.

3. Stir in 2 to 3 tablespoon of water.

4. Add chopped parsley and stir well.

5. Heat oil to in a medium skillet over medium-high heat.

Dredge each artichoke in flour.

6. When oil is hot, fry artichokes, a few at a time, turning occasionally, about 2 minutes.

7. Remove artichoces, drain on the kitchen paper towels, and sprinkle with salt.

Serve with sesame sauce.

54

Fried Squid with Mustard Sauce

Servings: 6

Cooking Times: 20 minutes

Ingredients

- 8 squids, cleaned

- 2 cups of milk

- For the sauce

- Juice from 2 lemons

- 4 Tbsp of yellow mustard

- 1/2 cup of extra virgin olive oil

- 2 Tbsp of fresh oregano finely chopped

- Salt and ground black pepper to taste

- 1/2 bunch of parsley finely chopped

Instructions

1. Cut squids into slices without to cut them completely.

2. Place squids in a large metal bowl with milk, and refrigerate over night.

3. Remove squids from the fridge and drain well.

4. In a bowl, whisk fresh lemon juice and the mustard.

5. Pour the olive oil and whisk until all ingredients combined well.

6. Add the oregano and the pepper and stir well.

7. Heat the oil in a large non-stick skillet over medium-high heat.

8. Fry squid until crisp or 1 to 2 minutes per side.

9. Transfer squid on a serving plate, cover with mustard sauce and sprinkle with parsley.

Pan-Fried Cod Patties

Servings: 3

Cooking Times: 35 minutes

Ingredients

- 1 lb of dried salt cod
- 1 cup of olive oil
- 1 clove garlic, minced
- 1 small yellow onion, minced
- 1 cup flour
- 1 tsp kosher salt, plus more to taste
- 1 egg from free-range chickens
- 2 Tbs unsalted butter, melted
- 2 tsp finely chopped cilantro
- Water

Instructions

1. Place cod in a saucepan and cover with cold water; bring to a boil over high heat and cook for 15 minutes.

2. Drain cod, return to saucepan, and repeat process twice more.

3. Transfer cod to a bowl and flake with a fork into small chunks; set aside.

4. Heat oil in a frying skillet over medium-high heat.

5. Add garlic and onion; cook until soft, about 5 minutes. Transfer to a bowl; set aside.

6. Whisk flour, salt, egg, and water in a bowl.

7. Stir cod, garlic and onion, butter, and cilantro together to form a thin batter.

8. Add 1 cup oil in a frying skillet and heat over high heat.

9. Pour about 1 tablespoon of batter into skillet; cook, flipping once, until golden brown, 1–2 minutes.

10. Using a spatula, transfer   patties to paper towels to drain.

Season with salt and serve hot.

Fried Mild Chili Peppers with Garlic

Servings: 6

Cooking Time: 15 minutes

Ingredients

- 1 cup of extra-virgin olive oil
- 1 lb of small mild chili peppers
- Salt to taste
- Fresh lemon juice
- 3 cloves of garlic sliced

Instructions

1. Heat extra-virgin olive oil in a large frying skillet over medium-high heat.

2. Add mild chili peppers and fry, turning often, until soft or about 15 minutes.

3. Transfer peppers to plate lined with kitchen paper, and generously season with salt.

4. Sprinkle with lemon juice and garlic and serve.

Savory Shrimp with Pancetta and Rosemary

Servings: 4

Cooking Times: 25 minutes

Ingredients

- 8 oz pancetta, finely chopped
- 1/4 cup olive oil
- 4 cloves garlic, thinly sliced
- 16 medium shrimp, deveined
- Kosher salt and freshly ground black pepper, to taste
- 1/2 cup white wine
- 2 sprigs rosemary, stemmed
- 1 medium tomato, cored, seeded, and finely chopped

Instructions

1. Heat pancetta and oil in a frying skillet over medium-high heat.

2. Cook until crisp, for about 6–8 minutes.

3. Using a slotted spoon, transfer pancetta to a plate lined with kitchen paper towel.

4. Add garlic to skillet, and saute for 1 minute.

5. Season shrimp with the salt and pepper; add to skillet.

6. Cook for about 2 to 3 minutes.

7. Add wine, rosemary, and tomato; cook until wine is reduced by half, 2–3 minutes.

8. Sprinkle with pancetta and serve.

Fried Green Beans with Ground Pork

Servings: 2

Cooking Times: 25 minutes

Ingredients

- 1 cup of olive oil
- 10 oz green beans, cut into pieces
- 2 oz ground pork
- 3 Tbsp of pickled mustard greens
- 1 Tbsp of red wine
- 1 Tbsp of soy sauce
- 1 tsp of toasted sesame oil
- Kosher salt and freshly ground black pepper, to taste

Instructions

1. Heat 2 tablespoon oil in a frying skillet over medium-high heat.

2. Add green beans, and cook, stirring often, until tender, about 5 minutes.

3. Transfer to a bowl, and set aside; return wok to high heat.

4. Add remaining oil, and then add ground pork. Stir for about 2 minutes.

5. Return beans to frying skillet along with greens, wine, and soy sauce, and cook, stirring, until heated through, about 2 to 3 minutes.

6. Remove from heat; stir in sesame oil, adjust seasoning to taste and serve.

Jolly Morning Egg Muffins

Servings: 6

Preparation Time: 35 minutes

Ingredients

- 6 large eggs from free-range chickens
- 1/4 cup of milk
- pinch of sea salt and black pepper
- 1 large red pepper, finely chopped
- 1 cup of fresh or frozen spinach
- 1/2 cup of shredded Cheddar cheese or Parmesan

Instructions

1. Preheat the oven to 375 F/ 185 C.
2. Grease the muffin tray.
3. In a bowl, whisk the eggs and the milk.
4. Season with the salt and pepper.
5. Add the pepper and continue to whisk.
6. Add chopped spinach and stir well.
7. Finally, add grated cheese and stir.
8. Pour the batter in a muffin tray 3/4 of the way full.
9. Bake for about 20 to 25 minutes.
10. Remove muffins from the tray and serve.
11. Keep refrigerated in an airtight container for one week.

Grilled Oyster Mushrooms

Servings: 4

Preparation Time: 20 minutes

Ingredients

- 3 garlic cloves, peeled and chopped
- Leaves from 1/4 bunch parsley, chopped
- 1/4 cup fruity olive oil
- Salt to taste
- 1 lb oyster mushrooms, cleaned and trimmed
- 1/2 lb white mushrooms, stemmed

Instructions

1. Preheat your grill (pellet, gas, charcoal) to HIGH according to manufacturer instructions.

2. Combine garlic, parsley, olive oil, and salt to taste in a small bowl.

3. Grill mushrooms without turning, basting often with parsley oil for about 5–10 minutes.

4. Serve hot or warm..

Grilled Halloumi Cheese

Servings: 4

Preparation Time: 15 minutes

Ingredients

- 1 lb of Haloummi cheese cut in slices
- 2 to 3 Tbs of olive oil
- 1 tsp of ground black pepper
- 1 Tbs of fresh basil finely chopped

Instructions

1. Preheat your grill (pellet, gas, charcoal) to HIGH.

2. Cut cheese into slices.

3. Sprinkle cheese with olive oil, pepper and fresh basil.

4. Arrange the cheese slices on a grill, and cook for about 2 minutes per side.

5. Serve hot and enjoy!

Sparkling Oyster Mignonette

Ingredients

- 3 cup prosecco or cava
- 1 cup of champagne vinegar
- 1 Tbs crushed peppercorns
- 1 medium onion finely chopped
- Salt and black pepper to taste

Instructions

1. In a bowl, combine all ingredients together, and let sit for 30 minutes.

2. Serve the mixture with oysters on the half shell.

Cauliflower "Rice" Salad with Fresh Herbs

Servings: 6

Total Time: 15 minutes

Ingredients

- 1   large head of cauliflower
- 1 tsp sea salt to taste
- 1 tsp fresh cilantro, finely chopped
- 1 tsp fresh parsley finely chopped
- 1/2 tsp fresh   tarragon finely chopped
- 1 cup water (for Instant Pot)
- 3 Tbs olive oil

Instructions

1. Rinse the cauliflower and trim off the leaves.

2. Break off any large outer leaves, and slice off the stem.

3. Cut into large florets.

4. Pour the water in your Instant Pot.

5. Insert the steamer and place the cauliflower on it.

6. Lock lid into place and set on the MANUAL setting for 3 minutes.

7. Use Quick Release - turn the valve from sealing to venting to release the pressure.

8. Remove the cauliflower to a plate, and break up with a potato masher.

9. Stir the oil and adjust seasonings to taste. Serve.

Finely Breaded Fish Sticks (Oven baked)

Servings: 4

Cooking Times: 30 minutes

Ingredients

- 1 fish fillet cut into strips
- 2 eggs from free-range chickens
- 1 cup of almonds, roughly chopped
- 1 tsp of oregano
- Sea salt to taste
- 2 - 3 Tbsp of flour
- 2 Tbs of olive oil for greasing
- juice of 1 lemon (serving)

Instructions

1. Preheat oven to 380 F/190 C.

2. Cut fish fillet into sticks.

3. In a bowl, whisk the eggs with the fork.

4. In a separate bowl, combine chopped almonds with oregano.

5. In a third bowl, combine the flour with salt.

6. Roll the fish sticks in a chopped almonds, then roll into the eggs, and finaly roll in a flour.

7. Place breaded fish sticks into a baking dish greased with the olive oil.

8. Bake for 15 - 20 minutes.

9. Serve hot with lemon wedges.

Insta- Egg and Ham Cake

Servings: 6

Cooking Times: 15 minutes

Ingredients

- 1 Tbs olive oil
- 6 free-range eggs
- 1 1/4 cups of milk
- table salt to taste
- 1/2 cup turkey ham cut into cubes
- 1 cup of water

Instructions

1. Grease a baking dish with olive oil; set aside.

2. Ina bowl, whisk eggs, milk and salt.

3. Add the ham and stir well.

4. Pour the egg mixture in your prepared baking dish.

5. Pour water in your Instant Pot, and insert the steamer basket or trivet.

6. Place the baking dish on the steamer basket or on the top of trivet.

7. Lock lid into place and set on the MANUAL setting for 5 minutes.

8. Use the Quick Release valve to let the pressure out.

9. Carefully, open the lid and transfer the cake on a serving platter.

Instant Brussels Sprouts and Bacon Salad

Servings: 4

Preparation Time: 15 minutes

Ingredients

- 3 Tbsp olive oil
- 1 1/2 lbs of Brussels sprouts
- 1 Tbsp of fresh basil leaves chopped
- 1 tsp of fresh thyme, chopped
- 1 tsp of fresh parsley, finely chopped
- 1 cup of fine chopped bacon
- salt and ground black pepper to taste
- 1/2 cup water

Instructions

1. Rinse the Brussels Sprouts in cold water to remove any dust or dirt.

2. With the knife, cut the tip of the stem and discard it.

3. Turn on your Instant Pot and pour the oil.

4. Place Brussels Sprouts in your Instant Pot with all remaining ingredients; toss to combine well.

5. Lock lid into place and set on the MANUAL setting for 4 minutes.

6. When the timer beeps, press "Cancel".

7. Use the Quick Release valve to let the pressure out.

8. Before serving drop some more olive oil and serve.

Instant Chicken and Endive Soup

Servings: 8

Preparation Time: 30 minutes

Ingredients

- 2 Tbsp olive oil
- 1 cup green onions
- 1 1/2 lbs   pastured raised chicken   thighs, skinless boneless
- 4 celery stalks, chopped
- 1 Tbsp dried oregano
- 1 endive head, cut into wide strips
- 1 tsp fennel seeds
- 8 cups of water
- Salt and pepper to taste

Instructions

1. Cut the chicken in a small cubes.

2. Press SAUTÉ button on your Instant Pot.

3. Sauté the chickens, green onions with a little salt about 5 minutes.

3. Add all remaining ingredients and stir well.

4. Lock lid into place and set on the SOUP/STEW on HIGH pressure for 12 minutes.

5. When the timer beeps, us Quick Release valve to let the pressure out.

6. Taste and adjust salt and pepper to taste.

7. Serve hot or warm..

Instant Mediterranean Lemon Octopus

Servings: 5

Preparation Time: 25 minutes

Ingredients

- 4 Tbs garlic-infused olive oil
- 3 lbs octopus cleaned, cut in cubes
- Kosher salt to taste
- 1/4 cup apple vinegar
- 1 tsp fresh chopped parsley
- 1 tsp oregano (or to taste)
- 4 Tbsp fresh lemon   juice

Instructions

1. Pour the oil in your Instant Pot.

2. Season the octopus with kosher salt to taste.

3. Place the octopus in your Instant Pot.

4. Add all remaining ingredients from the list.

5. Lock lid into place and set on the MANUAL setting for 10 minutes.

6. Use Natural Release - 10 to 15 minutes to depressurize naturally.

7. Open the lid and transfer the octopus with liquids into serving plate.

8. Sprinkle with lemon juice and serve.

Italiana Mushrooms Frittata

Servings: 6, Preparation Time: 45 minutes

Ingredients

- 6 large eggs
- 1/2 cup of parmesan cheese, shredded
- 1 onion finely chopped
- 1 tsp of fresh chopped thyme
- 1 tsp of fresh chopped basil
- 4 Tbs of fresh cream
- 3 Tbsp of fresh butter
- 3/4 lb of button mushrooms
- salt and ground black pepper to taste

Instructions

1. Preheat oven to 400 F/200 C.

2. Grease with butter an non-stick baking pan; set aside.

3. Wash the mushrooms to remove any dirt; cut into slices.

4. Peel the onion and slice it thinly.

5. In a bowl, whisk eggs together with two tablespoons of Parmesan, salt, thyme and 6. cream.

7. Heat butter In a frying pan over medium heat.

8. Sauté the onion with a pinch of salt and pepper until soft.

9. Add the mushrooms and cook for further two minutes; stir.

10. Remove from the heat and allow it to cool for 5 minutes.

11. Combine the egg mixture with the mushrooms and shallot and stir well.

12. Pour the mixture in a prepared pan and bake for 30 minutes.

13. Allow it to cool down before serving.

Spiced Chicken and Tomato Kebob

Servings: 4, Preparation Time: 45 minutes

Ingredients

- 1 cup plain yogurt
- 1 cup of fresh lime juice
- 2 Tbs of olive oil
- 2 Tbs of orange zest
- 1 Tbs of ground cumin
- Kosher salt and ground black pepper
- 2 tsp of saffron
- 1 tsp of ground coriander
- 6 cloves garlic, minced
- 1 large onion, finely sliced
- 2 lb boneless and skinless chicken
- 4 plum tomatoes, peeled
- 2 lemon, sliced

Instructions

1. In a bowl, stir together yogurt, juice, oil, zest, cumin, salt, pepper, saffron, coriander, garlic, and onion.

2. add chicken, and toss to coat. Chill for 4 hours.

3. Preheat your grill (pellet, gas, charcoal) to HIGH according to manufacturer instructions.

4. Skewer chicken on 4 metal skewers, and skewer tomatoes lengthwise on another skewer.

5. Grill chicken and tomatoes, turning often, until tomatoes about about 10 minutes.

Serve with lemon slices.

Keto "Fattoush" Salad

Servings: 4

Ingredients

- 1 onion, thinly sliced
- 1 head iceberg lettuce, chopped into bite-size pieces
- 2 cucumbers, sliced
- 3/4 cup of cherry tomatoes halved
- 2 Tbs of dried mint
- Dressing
- 1 cup of olive oil
- 2 Tbsp of lemon juice , freshly squeezed
- 1 tsp of garlic powder
- 2 pinches Kosher salt and freshly ground black pepper, to taste

Instructions

1. In a large salad bowl add onion, iceberg lettuce, cucumber, mint and cherry tomatoes.

2. Whisk all ingredients for dressing and pour over salad; toss to combine.

Chicken and Zucchini Goulash

Servings: 5, Preparation Time: 1 hour

Ingredients

- 1 Tbs of chicken fat melted
- 1 onion finely sliced
- 2 cloves of garlic
- 2 zucchini sliced
- 1 bell pepper sliced
- 1 cup of grated tomatoes
- 1 lb of chicken thighs boneless
- 1 cup of water
- 1/2 cup of beef broth
- salt and ground black pepper to taste
- 1/2 tsp of cumin
- 2 Tbs of fresh parsley finely chopped

Instructions

1. Heat the chicken fat in   frying skillet over medium-high heat.

2. Add the onion and garlic and sauté with the pinch of salt for about 3 to 4 minutes; stir.

3. Add zucchini, bell peppers and grated tomatoes; stir and simmer for 3 minutes stirring occasionally.

4. Add the chicken meat and season with the salt and pepper; cook for about 4 to 5 minutes.

5. Pour water and the broth, cumin and parsley, cover and cook for 30 to 35 minutes over medium-low heat.

6. Taste and adjust the seasonings.

7. Serve hot or warm..

Traditional Pancakes

Servings: 6

Preparation Time: 15 minutes

Ingredients

- 1 1/2 cup of flour
- 1 tsp of baking soda
- pinch of sugar
- pinch of salt
- 2 eggs from free-range chickens
- 1/2 cup of milk
- 1 tsp of vanilla extract
- Olive oil for baking (or coconut)

Instructions

1. In a bowl, combine the flour, baking soda, sugar and the pinch of salt.

2. In a separated bowl, whisk the eggs with milk and vanilla extract.

3. Add the flour mixture and stir until combined well.

4. Heat the oil in a large frying skillet.

5. Pour batter with the spoon to form pancakes; fry for 3 minutes or until bubbles form on top.

6. Flip the pancake and fry for about two minutes.

7. Transfer the pancake to the serving plate.

Delicious Shrimp-Eggplant Curry Stew

Servings: 3

Preparation Time: 30 minutes

Ingredients

- 3 Tbsp dried shrimp, rinsed
- 1 (1") piece ginger, peeled and thinly sliced
- 4 cloves garlic, peeled
- 1 cup of green onions, thinly sliced
- 3/4 cup of olive oil
- 1 tsp paprika
- 1 tsp of ground turmeric
- 3 eggplants, peeled,   and cut into cubes

Instructions

1. Soak shrimp in 1 cup boiling water until softened, 8–10 minutes.

2. Drain and transfer to a food processor; add ginger and purée into a smooth paste.

3. Transfer to a bowl and set aside.

4. Add garlic and green onion to food processor and purée into a smooth paste; set aside.

5. Heat half the oil in a frying skillet over medium-high heat.

6. Fry shrimp paste until fragrant, 2–3 minutes. Transfer to a bowl; set aside.

7. Add remaining oil to pan; fry garlic paste, the paprika, and turmeric, stirring 2. 2. constantly, until fragrant, 1–2 minutes.

8. Return shrimp paste to pan; add eggplant and 2 cups water; boil.

9. Reduce heat to medium; simmer, stirring occasionally, until eggplant is tender, 8–10 minutes. Serve with rice on the side.

Lemonato Parmesan Dip

Servings: 4

Preparation Time: 10 minutes

Ingredients

- 1 1/4 cups mayonnaise
- 3 cups of grated Parmesan cheese
- 2 Tbs of fresh lemon juice
- 2 tsp ofDijon mustard
- 2 clove garlic, mashed into a paste
- Zest of 1 lemon
- Kosher salt and freshly ground black pepper, to taste

Instructions

1. Stir all ingredients together in a bowl until smooth.

2. Keep refrigerated.

Shepards Breaded Cauliflower

Servings: 4, Preparation time: 25 minutes

Ingredients

- 1 large head of cauliflower cut into   florets
- 1 1/4 cups of flour
- 1 Tbsp of lemon zest
- 1 tsp of turmeric
- 1 tsp of cayenne
- Kosher salt and freshly ground black pepper,to taste
- 5 eggs
- Olive oil, for frying
- Roughly chopped parsley, for garnish
- Lemon wedges for serving

Instructions

1. Bring a large pot of salted water to a boil; add cauliflower and cook until just tender, about 5 minutes.

2. Remove cauliflower into colander to drain; dry completely with paper towels.

3. Heat oil in a deep frying skillet.

4. Stir together flour, zest, turmeric, cayenne, salt and pepper to a shallow baking dish.

5. Whisk eggs in a bowl.

6. Dip cauliflower in flour (working in batches), , then egg, and once again in flour.

7. Fry, flipping as needed until golden and crisp or about 1 minute.

8. Transfer to paper towels to drain; season with salt and pepper.

9. Garnish with parsley and serve with lemon wedges.

Mackerel and Cauliflower Soup

Servings: 6

Cooking Times

Total Time: 45 minutes

Ingredients

- 1/4 cup of olive oil
- 1 onion finely chopped
- 2 cloves of garlic, chopped
- 1 carrot sliced
- 3 tsp of fresh parsley, chopped
- 2 fresh tomatoes, peeled and diced
- 1/2 tsp sweet paprika
- 3 1/2 cup water
- 1 1/2 lb mackerel, boneless
- 2 cups of cauliflower florets, diced
- salt and freshly ground pepper to taste

Instructions

1. Cut fish it into small chunks.

2. Heat the olive oil in a frying pan, and sauté the onion and garlic until soft.

3. Add the carrot and parsley and sauté for 2 minutes; stir.

4. Add tomatoes and cook, stirring often, about 10 - 15 minutes.

5. Add sweet paprika and pour in the water.

6. Bring soup to boil, cover the lid and simmer about 15 minutes.

7. At the end, add the fish and cauliflower and let it cook for a 20 minutes.

8. Adjust salt and pepper to taste.

9. Serve hot or warm..

"Airy" Vanilla Meringues

Servings: 16

Preparation Time: 1 hour and 40 minutes

Ingredients

- 6 egg whites
- 3/4 lb of granulated sugar
- 1 tsp of powdered vanilla
- a pinch of salt

Instructions

1. Preheat oven to 200 F/100 C.

2. In a bowl, whisk egg whites until frothy and firm.

3. In a mixing bowl, add the vanilla and   a pinch of salt.

4. Then, gradually start adding sugar mixing continuously with an electric mixer (about 5 to 7 minutes).

5.Use two teaspoons to spoon meringue onto lined trays.

6.Bake for 1 1/2   hours.

7. Serve.

Marinated Sardines with Caper

Servings: 4

Preparation Time: 20 minutes

Inactive Time: 30 minutes

Ingredients

- 1 lb fresh sardines
- Salt and ground pepper
- 2 Tbs wine vinegar
- 1 tsp fresh oregano
- 3 Tbs olive oil
- 1/2 cup of caper
- 1 lemon sliced

Instructions

1. Rinse and clean sardines well.

2. Remove the central bone and heads.

3. Arrange sardines in a pan and season the salt well.

4. Cover and place sardines in refrigerator for about 30 minutes.

5. When ready, remove sardines, sprinkle with the oil, vinegar and oregano.

6. Serve sardines on the plate with lime, adding some olive oil next to the capers.

Marinated Venison Tenderloin on Grill

Servings: 4

Preparation Time: 20 minutes

Inactive Time: 2 hours

Ingredients

- Marinade
- 3 Tbs Worcestershire sauce
- 3 Tbs fresh lemon juice
- 1 Tbs hot pepper sauce
- 1 tsp red pepper flakes
- 1 tsp salt and freshly ground black pepper
- 1 tsp sage leaves
- 2 lbs of venison tenderloin

Instructions

1. Whisk all ingredients for marinade, and pour into a resealable plastic bag.

2. Add venison tenderloin, coat with the marinade, toss,   and seal the bag.

3. Refrigerate for at least 2 hours.

4. Preheat your grill (pellet, gas, charcoal) to HIGH according to manufacturer instructions.

5. Remove venison tenderloin from marinade and par dry on kitchen towel. Discard remaining marinade.

6. Grill for about 7 - 8 minutes per side or until thermometer inserted reach 150 degrees F (65 degrees C).

7. Remove from grill and let rest 10 minutes before serving.

Finely Spinach "Meatballs"

Servings: 4

Cooking Times

Preparation Time: 25 minutes

Ingredients

- 1/4 cup olive oil
- 1 small onion finely chopped
- 3/4 lb minced beef meat
- 1 lb frozen spinach, thawed and drained
- 1 tsp fresh basil finely chopped
- 1 free-range egg
- 3 Tbsp of almond flour
- 1/4 tsp sweet paprika powder
- salt and ground pepper to taste

Instructions

1. Heat the oil in a frying pan over medium-strong heat.

2. Sauté the onion with a pinch of salt for 3 - 4 minutes; stir occasional.

3. Add the spinach and sauté   for 3 minutes.
Remove the mixture from heat, and let cool on room temperature.

4. Combine the spinach and meat mixture with egg, basil, and salt and pepper.

5. Using your hands, knead until all ingredients are combined well.

6. Sprinkle flour and sweet paprika, and knead again.

7. Form the mixture into patties or balls.

8. Fry patties in a hot frying pan (with or without oil) for 2-3 minutes per side.

9. Serve hot or warm..

Mediterranean Zucchini and Feta Casserole

Servings: 6

Preparation Time: 3 hours and 20 minutes

Ingredients

- 2 Tbsp olive oil
- 4 large zucchinis
- 1 onion, finely chopped
- 1 1/2 cup feta cheese
- 4 eggs
- seasoned salt and pepper to taste

Instructions

1. Pour the olive oil in your Slow Cooker and dump the scallion; season with the pinch of seasoned salt.

2. Slice the zucchinis and place in Slow Cooker.

3. Whisk eggs with Feta cheese, and salt and pepper.

4. Pour the egg mixture into Slow Cooker over zucchini slices.

5. Cover and cook on HIGH for 3 hours.

6. Serve hot or warm..

Oven-baked Zucchini Patties

Servings: 12

Preparation Time: 40 minutes

Ingredients

- 1 lb zucchini, grated , squeezed of excess moisture
- 2 eggs from free-range chickens
- 1 green onion finely chopped
- 3 Tbs of leeks (bulb) finely chopped
- 1 1/2 Tbs of fresh herbs (dill and mint)
- 1 Tbs of granulated stevia sweetener
- 1/3 cup of almond flour
- 2 Tbs grated walnuts
- Sea salt and freshly ground black pepper
- 1/4 cup of olive oil (or garlic-infused olive oil)

Instructions

1. Preheat oven to 360 F/180 C.

2. Oil a large baking pan and line with the parchment paper; set aside.

3. Grate tucchini, stir and leave in colander to drain   for 15 minutes.

4. Transfer yucchini in a bowl, add all remaining ingredients and stir well.

5. Form the mixture into 12 patties.

6. Place zucchini patties into prepared baking pan and sprinkle with olive oil.

7. Bake for about 20-25 minutes.

8. Serve immediately or keep refrigerated in a closed containers until serving.

Mediterranean Deviled Eggs

Servings: 6

Preparation Time: 20 minutes

Ingredients

- 6 hard-boiled eggs
- 3 Tbsp sour cream
- 2 Tbsp anchovy paste
- 1 tsp Dijon mustard
- Kosher salt and freshly ground black pepper, to taste
- 12 white anchovy filets, rinsed and drained
- 1 Tbsp minced chives
- 1 Tbsp of fresh sage finely chopped
- 2 sprigs rosemary finely chopped

Instructions

1. Halve eggs lengthwise; set whites aside.

2. Place yolks in a small bowl, and mash it; stir in sour cream, paste, mustard, and salt and pepper.

3. Transfer mixture to a small piping bag; pipe into egg white cavities, and then place an anchovy filet over each egg.

4. Sprinkle with chives, sage and rosemary.

5. Serve.

Hearty Broccoli & Zucchini Soup

Servings: 6

Preparation Time: 35 minutes

Ingredients

- 1/4 cup of olive oil
- 2 leek, chopped
- 1 1/2 lbs of fresh broccoli, cut into flower clusters
- 2 zucchini finely slices
- 1 carrot finely chopped
- 4 cups of water
- 1/2 tsp of Dill
- 1/2 tsp of marjoram
- 1/2 half a cup of almond milk
- salt and ground black pepper to taste

Instructions

1. Heat the oil in a large frying skillet over medium-high heat.

2. Sauté the leek with the pinch of salt for 5 to 7 minutes.

3. Add broccoli, zucchini, and carrot; sauté for 3 to 4 minutes.

4. Pour water and season with dill, marjoram, and the salt and pepper; stir.

5. Cover and simmer for about 15 minutes.

6. Transfer soup to the blender and pour the almond milk; blend until smooth and creamy.

7. Serve warm.

Asiago Cheese Crisps

Servings: 10

Cooking Time: 35 minutes

Ingredients

- 1 lb of asiago cheese
- 1 Tbs of almond flour
- Extra-virgin olive oil

Instructions

1. Combine cheese with flour in a medium bowl. Mix thoroughly.

2. Grease a large skillet with oil, then place over medium-low heat.

3. Spoon 2 tablespoon of cheese onto heated skillet.

4. Allow cheese to melt and edges to turn golden brown.

5. Cook for about 3 minutes, then turn with a spatula and continue cooking for further 2 minutes.

6. Serve immediatelly.

Piquant Razor Clams

Servings: 4

Preparation Time: 20 minutes

Ingredients

- 2/3 cup of olive oil
- 4 cloves garlic, finely chopped
- 3–4 dried chily peppers, crumbled
- 1 1/2 lbs of razor clams, rinsed thoroughly
- 1 cup of white wine
- 1 1/4 cups loosely packed flat-leaf parsley leaves, minced
- 1 pinch Kosher salt or to taste

Instructions

1. Heat oil, garlic, and chiles in a frying skillet over medium heat.

2. Cook, stirring occasionally, for about 5 to 6 minutes.

3. Increase heat to high, add razor clams and wine; cook, covered, until clams are just cooked through, about 3 minutes.

4. Add parsley and season with salt; toss razor clams to coat with sauce.

5. Transfer clams to a serving platter and drizzle with remaining sauce.

Creamy Meatballs (Oven Baked)

Servings: 4

Preparation Time: 30 minutes

Ingredients

- 2 Tbs fresh butter
- 1 scallion, finely chopped
- 1 egg organic
- 3/4 lb of ground beef
- 1/4 lb of minced pork
- 1 tsp of natural sweetener like stevia
- Salt and ground pepper to taste
- 1/2 tsp of nutmeg
- 2 Tbsp of olive oil
- 3/4 cup of cooking cream
- 1/4 cup of bone broth
- 2 tsp fresh dill finely chopped
- 2 tsp of fresh parsley finely chopped

Instructions

1. Preheat oven to 350 F/175   C.

2. Grease one baking dish with the butter set aside.

3. Combine all remaining ingredients in a large bowl.

4. Knead the mixture until well combined.

5. From the mixture shape meatballs; place them in oiled baking dish.

6. Heat oil in a pan over medium heat; add the cooking cream and the bone broth.

7. Cook the mixture for 2 - 3 minutes.

8. Pour the cooking cream mixture over meatballs, sprinkle with fresh dill and parsley.

9. Cover with foil and bake for 20 minutes or until meatballs are cooked trough.

10. Serve hot or warm..

Anchovies Stuffed Cherry Peppers

Servings: 10

Ingredients

- 5 oz canned tuna in olive oil, drained

- 8 anchovies in oil, drained

- 1 1 cups extra-virgin olive oil

- 1 cup of almond flour

- 2 Tbs capers, minced

- 2 Tbs finely chopped parsley

- Kosher salt and freshly ground black pepper, to taste

- 1 32-oz. jar red, hot cherry peppers, drained, rinsed, and stemmed (jar reserved)

Instructions

1. Chop tuna and anchovies; stir with oil, almond flour, capers, parsley, and salt and pepper in a bowl.

2. Fill each pepper with tuna mixture.

3. Transfer to reserved jar; pour remaining oil over peppers.

4. Chill for at least 8 hours to marinate.

Roasted Partridges with Herbs

Servings: 6

Preparation Time: 35 minutes

Ingredients

- 4 partridges whole
- 2 Tbs sunflower oil
- 2 Tbs fresh rosemary
- 1 Tbs fresh parsley
- 1 Tbs lemon juice
- 1 tsp fresh sage
- Salt and ground pepper to taste

Instructions

1. Preheat oven to 360 F/180 C.

2. Put the partridge breast-down on the work surface and cut up both sides of the backbone with strong scissors.

3. Place the partrige in a greased baking dish.

4. In a bowl, combine oil, rosemary, parsley, lemon juice, sage and salt and pepper to taste.

5. Pour marinade over the birds.

6. Place the roasting dish in the oven and let the partridges cook, covered, for roughly 25 minutes.

7. From time to time, open the oven and baste partridges with marinade.

8. Remove the birds from the oven, and let rest 10 minutes before slicing and serving.

Artichoke and Asparagus Salad (Crock Pot)

Servings: 6

Preparation Time: 8 hours

Ingredients

- 2 Tbsp of olive oil (or garlic-infused olive oil)
- 8 medium fresh artichokes
- 1 lb of fresh, tender, green asparagus, cut into pieces
- 1 tsp of fresh oregano finely chopped
- 1 tsp of fresh rosemary
- 1 tsp of fresh sage chopped
- 2 cups of water (lukewarm)
- Salt and white pepper to taste

Instructions

1. Grease your Crock Pot with oil and add asparagus and artichokes; season with a pinch of salt.

2. Season with herbs and pour water.

3. Cover and cook on LOW setting for 6 - 8 hours or until artichokes are tender.

4. Adjust seasonings and serve hot.

Perfect Roasted Duck Breasts

Servings: 2

Preparation Time: 20 minutes

Inactive Time: 8 hours

Ingredients

- 2 duck breasts (along with the skin)
- Kosher salt
- 1/4 cup garlic-infused olive oil
- 1/4 cup of apple- wine vinegar
- ¼ cup of fresh orange juice
- 1 sprig of rosemary
- 1 sprig of fresh thyme

Instructions

1. Cut with a sharp knife the duck skin, fat, and the meat.

2. Generously   rub well the salt over the whole   surface of ducks breast.

3. Place the duck in a deep container.

4. Whisk the olive oil, vinegar, orange juice, rosemary, thyme and salt.

5. Pour marinade over duck and refrigerate for 8 hours.

6. Preheat oven to 420 F/210C.

7. Grease a baking dish and place the duck breasts.

8. Arrange a duck breasts with the skin side up, with a distance one from the another.

9. Bake for 6 - 10 minutes for medium rare.

10. Remove the duck from the oven and let it rest for 10 minutes before serving.

Pork Rind Breaded Shrimp

Servings: 4

Preparation Time: 25 minutes

Ingredients

- 2 Tbs of olive oil
- 6 oz pork rinds
- 1/4 cup of grated Parmesan or Cheddar
- 1/2 tsp of sweet paprika
- 1/2 tsp of garlic powder
- 1 tsp of chili powder
- 1 tsp of onion powder
- 1/2 tsp of dried oregano
- 1 tsp of dried thyme
- Sea salt and freshly ground black pepper
- 2 large eggs
- 1 1/2 lb of shrimp cleaned and deveined

Instructions

1. Preheat oven to 450F/220 C.

2. Grease a large baking sheet with olive oil.

3. Crush pork rinds in a food processor.

4. Transfer crushed pork rinds to a bowl and combine together with all remaining ingredients (except eggs and shrimp).

5. In a bowl, whisk the eggs with a pinch of salt.

6. Dredge shrimp in eggs, and then coat in pork rind mixture.

7. Lay breaded shrimp into prepared baking sheet.

8. Bake for 10 to 12 minutes.

9. Serve hot or warm..

Quick and Easy Garlic Chicken

Servings: 4

Preparation Time: 30 minutes

Ingredients

- 4 chicken breasts boneless and skinless
- 6 garlic cloves, minced
- 4 Tbsp of coconut aminos
- 2 Tbsp of olive oil
- herbs and spices to a taste

Instructions

1. Preheat oven to 450°F.

2. Line a baking dish or cookie sheet with parchment paper, and lightly brush with oil.

3. In a frying pan, sauté garlic with the oil until tender.

4. Remove from heat and stir in coconut aminos.

5. Add herbs and spices as desired.

6. Place the chicken breasts in a prepared baking dish and cover with the garlic mixture.

7. Add salt and pepper to taste.

8. Bake uncovered for 15-30 minute.

Pork Tenderloin with Button Mushrooms

Servings: 6

Preparation Time: 25 minutes

Ingredients

- 1 1/2 lbs of pork tenderloin cut into pieces
- 1/2 cup of olive oil
- 1 lb of raw mushrooms
- 1 green onion finely chopped
- 2 garlic cloves
- Lemon juice from 2 lemons
- 1 tsp of lemon zest
- 1 tsp of curry
- Salt and ground black pepper
- 1 Tbs of mustard
- 1/2 cup of bone broth (optional)
- 1/2 cup of white wine
- 1 Tbs of almond flour
- 1/2 cup of water

Instructions

1. Cut the pork tenderloin into pieces and season generously with the salt and pepper; set aside.

2. Heat half of the olive oil in a large frying skillet over moderate heat; sauté the mushrooms for 3 miutes.

3. Add finely chopped green onion and garlic and stir until soft.

4. Season with the salt the pepper; stir for 3 - 4 minutes, and remove from pan in a bowl.

5. In the same frying pan or saucepan, add the remaining olive oil and sauté the tenderloin for 2 - 3 minutes.

6. Pour the wine, and add again the mushrooms mixture along with lemon zest, lemon juice, mustard, bone broth (if used) and curry; stir.

7. Dissolve the almond flour in a 1/2 cup of water and pour in a skillet.

8. Stir with a wooden spoon and cook for 10 minutes at medium-low heat.

9. Serve hot or warm..

Insta-Spiced Zucchini with Nutmeg

Servings: 4

Total Time: 25 minutes

Ingredients

- 2 lbs of zucchini, sliced
- 3/4 cup of water
- 2 Tbs of fresh butter, grass-fed, unsalted
- 1/2 tsp of grated nutmeg
- 2 tsp fresh marjoram leaves, chopped
- Salt and pepper to taste

Instructions

1. Place all ingredients in your Instant Pot.

2. Lock lid into place and set on the MANUAL setting at LOW for 2 minutes.

3. When the timer beeps, press "Cancel" and carefully flip the Quick Release valve to let the pressure out.

4. Taste, adjust seasonings to taste and serve.

Marinated Sour Radicchio di Treviso

Servings: 4

Preparation Time: 35 minutes

Ingredients

- 6 heads of treviso radicchio
- 1 cup of white wine vinegar
- 3 cups of water
- 5 black peppercorns
- 1 tsp salt
- 1 bay leaf
- 1 cup extra-virgin olive oil
- Salt and freshly ground black pepper
- Finely grated hard-cooked egg

Instructions

1. Rinse, and clean any whitered outer leaves from radicchio.

2. Quarter heads lengthwise and set aside.

3. Combine the vinegar, water, peppercorns, salt, and bay leaf in a large pot and bring to a boil.

4. Blanch radicchio wedges, a few at a time, for 1–2 minutes.

5. Pat dry with a kitchen paper towel.

6. Arrange wedges in layers in a glass or ceramic dish.

7. Sprinkle with olive oil, cover with plastic wrap, and refrigerate overnight.

8. Bring radicchio to room temperature, season with salt and pepper, and slice.

9. Serve garnished with finely grated hard-cooked egg.

Homemade Broccoli and Mustard Dip

Servings: 4

Preparation Time: 15 minutes

Ingredients

- 1 lb of broccoli, cooked
- 2 Tbsp   mustard
- 1/2 cup of olive oil
- 1/2 cup lemon juice
- 1 clove of garlic
- 3 Tbsp of fresh basil finely chopped
- Salt and freshly pepper to taste

Instructions

1. Boil water in a large pot with a salt.

2. Add the broccoli florets and cook for about 2   minutes.

3. Remove broccoli with a slotted spoon and plunge in the cold water.

4. Remove broccoli in a colander to drain.

5. Place all ingredients in a fast speed blender.

6. Blend until all ingredients combine well.

7. Taste and adjust salt and pepper to taste

8. Serve.

Herbed Beef Tenderloin with Bacon

Servings: 6

Preparation Time: 1 hour and 25 minutes

Ingredients

- 2 lb beef tenderloin roast
- 6 slices of bacon
- 2 Tbsp basil leaves, chopped
- 1/4 cup of fresh parsley finely and chopped
- 2 Tbsp of   fresh oregano finely chopped
- 2 Tbsp of fresh rosemary finely chopped
- 3 cloves of garlic, crushed
- 2 Tbsp of olive oil
- Salt and ground pepper to taste

Instructions

1. Preheat oven to 425 F/210 C.

2. Season the beef roast with salt the and pepper; set aside.

3. In bowl, combine chopped parsley, basil, oregano, rosemary, garlic and oil.

4. Press the herb mixture onto top and sides of beef.

5. Add the meat in a greased roasting pan.

6. Roll the bacon slices over top of beef and place in a roasting pan.

7. Bake for about 45 to 50 minutes.

8. Remove beef from oven, cover with foil and let sit   about 15 minutes before slicing.

9. Serve.

Roasted Chicken Breast with Fragrant Herbs

Servings: 4

Preparation Time: 40 minutes

Ingredients

- 2 lbs   chicken breasts, bone-in skin-on
- 3 Tbs garlic-infuse olive oil
- 1 tsp of fresh thyme finely chopped
- 1 tsp of fresh rosemary, finely chopped
- 1 tsp of fresh basil, finely chopped
- 2 Tbsp fresh lemon juice
- salt and ground black pepper per taste
- 1/2 cup water
- Lemon wedges, for serving

Instructions

1. Preheat oven to 400° F/200C.

2. Season generously chicken with the salt and pepper.

3. Grease a large baking dish with oil.

4. Place the chicken in a baking dish, and sprinkle with fresh rosemary, basil and thyme, and pour lemon juice and water.

5. Bake for 25 to 30 minutes.

6. Remove chicken from oven and let sit for 10 minutes.

7. Serve with lemon wedges.

Baked Breaded Zucchini with Fresh Dill

Servings: 4

Preparation Time: 30 minutes

Ingredients

- 4 to 5 zucchini, cleaned and sliced
- 3 Tbs of almond milk
- 4 Tbs of ground almonds
- 2 Tbs of almond flour
- 2 Tbs of water
- Salt and ground pepper to taste
- 1/2 cup of extra-virgin olive oil
- 2 to 3 Tbs of fresh dill, finely chopped (for servings)

Instruction

1. Preheat oven to 350 F/175 C.

2. Grease a large baking sheet with olive oil.

3. Wash, clean and slice zucchini lengthwise. Season with the salt and let sit in a colander for 15 to 20 minutes.

5. In a large bowl, combine together, almond milk, oil, ground almonds and flour, and two tablespoons of water. Season with the salt and pepper and stir well.

6. Arrange zucchini slices into a prepared baking dish, and pour almond mixture over them. Bake for about 15 to 17 minutes or until zucchini gets a golden brown color.

8. Sprinkle with fresh dill and serve hot.

Creamy Salmon Dip

Servings: 8

Preparation Time: 25 minutes

Ingredients

- 8 oz boneless skinless salmon filet
- 3 Tbs lemon juice
- 2 Tbs olive oil
- 1 pinch Kosher salt and freshly ground black pepper, to taste
- 2 Tbsp fresh creme
- 1 Tbsp finely chopped parsley
- 1 medium shallot, finely chopped (1 cup)
- Zest of one lemon

Instruction

1. Preheat oven to 375 F/185 C.

2. Place salmon in a baking dish and drizzle with 2 tablespoon of lemon juice, olive oil, salt, and pepper.

3. Bake 15 minutes until cooked through; set aside to cool.

4. When salmon is cool enough to handle, combine with creme, parsley, shallot, remaining lemon juice, and zest.

5. Season with salt and pepper.

Sardine Fritters

Servings: 6

Preparation Time: 15 minutes

Ingredients

- 2 large eggs
- 3/4 cup of almond flour
- 1/2 cup of cold sparkling water
- salt and ground black pepper to taste
- 2 Tbs of fresh chopped parsley
- 1 can (15 oz)   of sardines
- Olive oil for frying

Instructions

1. In a bowl, beat the eggs and slowly add the almond flour constantly beating.

2. Pour the sparkling water, season with the salt and pepper, and chopped parsley.

3. Whisk until get a thick batter.

4. Put sardines in a bowl, rinse gently under running water and drain in a colander.

5. Add sardines to the batter and stir with a spoon.

6. Heat oil in a deep frying skillet, and fry fritters for one minute on each side.

7. Serve hot or warm..

Italian Braised Celery with Crispy Bacon

Servings: 4

Preparation Time: 35 minutes

Ingredients

- 3 oz bacon, cut into thin sticks
- 1 cup of olive oil
- 1 large onion finely sliced
- 2 lb celery stalks, trimmed and cut diagonally
- 3 tomatoes, pealed and grated
- 1 cup of water
- Salt and ground black pepper to taste

Instructions

1. Heat the non-stick frying skillet and fry bacon until crisp.

2. Transfer bacon with slotted spoon to paper towels to drain; set aside.

3. Heat the olive in a frying pan on medium-high heat.

4. Saute onion with a pinch of salt, stirring occasionally for about 3 to 4 minutes.

5. Add celery, tomatoes, 1 cup of water, and season with the salt and pepper.

6. Cover and cook, stirring occasionally, until celery is very tender, about 15 to 20 minutes.

7. Serve hot with crispy bacon.

Spicy Cayenne Jumbo Shrimp

Servings: 4

Cooking Time: 45 minutes

Ingredients

- 1/2 cup of extra-virgin olive oil
- 6 cloves of garlic, peeled
- 2 Tbsp of fresh parsley, minced
- 1 cup sliced almonds, toasted
- 2 cups of bone broth
- 1 bay leaf
- 1/2 tsp of cayenne pepper
- Salt and freshly ground black pepper
- 16 jumbo shrimp, unpeeled

Instructions

1. Heat oil in a large skillet over medium-low heat.

2. Add crushed garlic and cook for 10 minutes.

3. Remove garlic with a slotted spoon and discard

4. Add minced garlic, parsley, almonds, and 3 tablespoon of stock in a high speed blender; blend to make a fine paste.

5. Pour remaining stock into skillet.

6. Add bay leaf, cayenne pepper, and season to taste with the salt and pepper.

7. Simmer over medium heat for 10 minutes.

8. Stir in garlic paste, stir well, adjust seasoning, and then add shrimp and simmer for about 5 minutes.

9. Discard bay leaf and serve hot.

Ground Beef Stuffed Peppers

Servings: 8

Preparation Time: 50 minutes

Ingredients

- 8 red peppers and yellow peppers
- 2 lbs of ground beef
- ½ onion, sliced
- 1 grated tomato
- 1 cup bone broth
- 1 tsp of red pepper
- Salt and fresh black pepper to taste
- 1 cup of chopped parsley
- 4 cloves of garlic, finely chopped
- 1 cup grated Parmesan cheese
- 1 cups of ground almonds

Instructions

1. Preheat oven to 380 F/190C.

2. Cut the pepper tops and carefully remove the stalks.

3. Clean good peppers and rinse.

4. In a baking dish, add the tomato sauce together with sliced onion, beef broth and stir well until a homogeneous mixture is done.

5. Place the peppers in the baking pan; set aside.

6. In a bowl, add ground meat and sprinkle with salt, chopped garlic, parsley, black pepper, grated parmesan cheese, tomato sauce and stir very well with a fork.

7. Add ground almonds and stir well.

8. Fill the peppers with the mixture.

9. Cover peppers with their tops.

10. Cover with foil and bake for 1 hour, then remove the foil and continue baking for 30 minutes.

11. Serve hot or warm..

Traditional Greek Chicken Skewers

Servings: 4

Preparation Time: 25 minutes

Ingredients

- ¼ cup of olive oil
- 4 Tbsp of lemon juice
- 1 tsp of sweet paprika
- 2 Tbsp of dried parsley
- Salt and ground black pepper to taste
- 8 boneless chicken thighs cut into pieces

Instructions

1. In a bowl, stir together the olive oil, lemon juice, paprika, parsley, and the salt and pepper.

2. Pour mixture over chicken and marinate for about 20-30 minutes.

3. Thread the chicken pieces on sticks.

4. Heat oil In a large frying pan on moderate- strong heat; fry the chicken skewers for 3-4 minutes each side or until lightly golden and cooked through.

5. Serve with chopped pita and tzatziki sauce.

Grilled Spiced Goat Chunks

Servings: 6

Cooking Times

Inactive Time: 4 hours and 15 minutes

Ingredients

- 3 lbs goat chunks chopped
- 2 tsp ground cumin
- 2 tsp sweet paprika
- 1/4 cup white vinegar
- 1/4 cup olive oil
- 1 lemon, juiced
- 3 tsp dried oregano

Instructions

1. In a large bowl or container combine all ingredients (except goat meat).

2. Add the goat to coat in marinade.

3. Cover with plastic wrap and refrigerate overnight.

4. Remove from refrigerather 45 minutes before cooking.

5. Preheat your grill or smoker to 225°F).

6. Grill until internal temperature reach 150 degrees F.

7. Serve warm.

Grilled Marinated Lamb Skewers in Foil

Servings: 6

Cooking Time: 20 minutes

Ingredients

- Marinade
- 1/3 cup olive oil
- juice of 1 lemon freshly squeezed
- 1/2 tsp cumin (optional)
- 1 tsp fresh thyme, chopped
- 1 tsp dried oregano
- 1 tsp rosemary sprig
- 1 tsp red pepper flakes (more or less to taste)
- salt and freshly ground pepper
- Meat3 lbs lamb legs cut into chunks

Instructions

1. Cut the meat into chunks and set aside.

2. Whisk together all ingredients for marinade.

3. Add the lamb meat in marinade and toss to coat.

4. Cover and refrigerate overnight.

5. Remove the meat from the marinade, and pat dry on paper towel.

6. Thread the lamb meat   onto a metal skewers.

7. Place skewers in foil and wrap well.

7. Preheat your grill (any) to HIGH.

8. Grill lamb 7-8 minutes for medium-rare (turning occasionaly) or when internal temperature reaches 150 degrees F.

9. Serve hot from the foil.

Smoked Halibut Fillets

Servings: 6

Cooking Times: 2 hours and 15 minutes

Ingredients

- 1 cup of virgin olive oil
- 1 Tbsp fresh rosemary (chopped)
- 1 Tbsp fresh parsley and cilantro, finely chopped
- 1/2 cup white vinegar
- 2 Tbsp lemon juice   (freshly squeezed)
- 4 halibut fillets

Instructions

1. Whisk the olive oil, fresh herbs and white vinegar in a container.

2. Add halibut fillets and toss to combine well.

3. Cover and marinate in refrigerator preferably overnight.

4. Remove halibut fillets from marinade and dry on paper towels for 30 minutes.

5. Preheat your Grill to reach 215 degrees Fahrenheit.

6. Smoke the fish for about 2 hours or more, until the internal temperature reaches 140 degrees F.

7. Turn once during cooking to avoid having the halibut fall apart.

8. Transfer to a large serving platter, pour with lemon juice over the fish and serve.

Shredded Turkey with Cabagge Salad

Servings: 4

Cooking Times: 10 minutes

Ingredients

- Salad ingredients
- 1 lb   cooked turkey breast, shredded
- 1/2   cabbage head, shredded
- 1/4 cup   green onions chopped
- 1/2 cup fresh celery finely chopped
- Salt to taste
- Dressing ingredients
- 1/4 cup mayonnaise (gluten-free, grain free, without honey)
- 3 Tbsp olive oil
- 1 tsp curry powder
- Salt and pepper to taste

Instructions

1. Combine all salad ingredients in shallow salad bowl; stir to combine well.

2. In a bowl, whisk the olive oil and mayonnaise until smooth.

3. Add the curry powder, and salt and pepper; continue to whisk until smooth.

4. Pour the dressing over the salad;   toss well.

5. Serve immediately or keep refrigerated.

Spicy Almond-Chili Breaded Olives

Servings: 4

Preparation Time: 15 minutes

Ingredients

- 24   olives pitted
- 1/2 cup of almond flour
- 1 tsp garlic powder
- 1/2 tsp of chilli powder
- 2 eggs from free-range chickens
- 1/2 cup of ground almonds
- 1/2 tsp ground paprika
- olive oil for frying

Instructions

1. Pat dry olives, and remove pits.

2. In a bowl, combine almond flour, powdered garlic and chili powder.

3. In the second bowl, whisk the eggs, and in the third bowl add ground almonds and paprika.

4. Roll olives into almond flour mixture, dip into eggs, and finally roll   into ground almonds mixture.

5. Heat the oil in a large frying skillet over high heat; fry olive for about one minute.

6. Serve hot or warm..

Fried Stuffed Squash Blossoms

Servings: 6

Preparation Time: 20 minutes

Ingredients

- 24 zucchini blossoms
- 3/4 lb of mozzarella diced
- 12 anchovy filets
- 4 eggs from free-range chickens
- 1 cup of almond flour
- Salt and freshly ground black pepper
- Olive oil

Instructions

1. Remove stems and stamens from zucchini blossoms; wash blossoms and pat dry.

2. Cut mozzarella into small dice, coarsely chop anchovy filets, and combine in a mixing bowl.

3. Stuff each blossom with mixture and twist petals to retain stuffing.

4. Whisk eggs in a small bowl.

5. Combine almond flour with freshly ground black pepper into fryinf pan.

6. Heat 2 1/2" vegetable oil in a skillet over high heat until very hot.

7. Dredge each stuffed blossom in flour; dip into eggs, turning to coat well, then dredge in seasoned flour.

8. Fry blossoms, turning frequently, until crisp, 3–5 minutes.

9. Drain on a kitchen paper towels, sprinkle with salt, and serve immediately.

Ultra Light Collard Greens Soup

Servings: 8

Preparation Time: 25 minutes

Ingredients

- 3 Tbs olive oil
- 2 green onions finely sliced (only green parts)
- 2 sweet potatoes, cut in cubes
- 2 bay leaves
- 8 cups water
- 1 lb raw collard greens (stem removed and leaves cut roughly)
- 4 cherry tomatoes
- 1 tsp fresh rosemary
- 1/2 tsp fresh thyme, finely chopped
- salt and pepper to taste

Instructions

1. Heat the oil in a large soup pot.

2. Sauté green onions with a pinch of salt for 2 minutes.

3. Add sweet potatoes, bay leaves and water.

3. Bring the mixture to a boil, and than reduce heat.

4. Cover the pot and cook until potatoes are very tender, about 10 -12 minutes.

5. Discard the bay leaves.

6. Transfer soup in a blender and blend until smooth.

7. Bring soup back to a gentle simmer and add the collard greens, fresh rosemary, thyme and tomatoes. Adjust salt and pepper to taste.

8. Cook about 2 - 4 minutes. Serve hot.

Mediterreanean Avgolemono   Chicken Soup

Servings: 8

Preparation Time: 1 hour and 35 minutes

Ingredients

- 1 whole chicken, cleaned
- 8 cups water
- 3 spring onions finely chopped
- 1 bunch of parsley finely chopped
- 1/4 cup fennel bulb, thinly sliced
- 1/2 tsp nutmeg grated
- 1/2 tsp allspice ground
- 4 Tbs bacon chopped
- salt and   pepper to taste
- 2 lemons (juice)
- 4 Free-range eggs

Instructions

1. Place the chicken in a large saucepan with enough water (to cover it).

2. Bring to boil, and than reduce heat to a gentle boil and cook for about 90 - 95 minutes, or until turkey meat is falling off of the bone.

3. When ready, remove the turkey from the water (keep two cups of broth).

4. Add all the ingredients to the broth, (except lemon and eggs) and leave to boil for about 10 minutes; turn off the heat.

5. Whisk the eggs in a bowl with the pinch of salt; pour the lemon juice; stir well.

6. Slowly, pour the egg-lemon mixture, stirring continuously, in a broth and stir until combined well.

7. Chop or shred one turkey breast, and add meat in a soup.

8. Taste and adjust seasonings.

9. Serve immediately.

Savory Eggs Baked in Tomatoes

Servings: 4

Preparation Time: 35 minutes

Ingredients

- 4 tomatoes
- 4 large eggs from free-range chickens
- 3 Tbsp of olive oil
- Salt and ground black pepper to taste
- 2 spring onions finely chopped

Instructions

1. Preheat oven to 360 F/180C.

2. Wash tomatoes and dry. Cut the tops and remove the pulp.

3. Season generously tomato cups with the salt and pepper.

4. Heat the olive oil in a frying pan and cook removed tomato pulp with a pinch of salt for 2 minutes.

5. Place the tomato cups in a greased baked dish, fill with fried tomato pulp, and crack an egg in each tomato; sprinkle the pinch of salt and pepper.

6. Place in oven and bake for 20 minutes.

7. Serve hot with chopped green onions.

Braised Wild Duck Breast with Vegetables

Servings: 4

Preparation Time: 40 minutes

Ingredients

- 3 Tbsp fresh   butter
- 1 scallion, roughly chopped
- 1 bunch kale, stalks removed, roughly chopped
- 2 cups   cauliflower chopped
- 2 tsp fresh rosemary chopped
- 2 Tbsp chives, finely chopped
- 1/2 cup fresh parsley leaves
- 2 Tbsp olive oil
- salt and pepper, to taste
- 4 wild duck breasts, skin removed

Instruction

1. Melt the butter in the frying pan over moderate-low heat.

2. Add the scallion, kale, and cook with pinch of salt for 5 minutes or until softened.

3. Add the cauliflower and chives and stir until well combined. Season with all herbs to taste.

4. Place the duck breasts on a plate and season each side with salt and pepper, and drizzle with oil.

5. Heat the oil in a large frying skillet over medium-high heat.

6. When hot, place the duck breasts, skin side down and gradually turn up the heat.

7. Fry for 5 - 10 minutes or until the skin is golden brown.

8. Serve hot with braised vegetables.

Printed in Great Britain
by Amazon